DISCOVERIN

HOW TO BEAT THE U.S. MARKET

BY M. G. ROBERTS

DISCLOSURES AND DISCLAIMER

Exchanged trade funds (ETFs) are baskets of securities that track recognized indexes and trade on an exchange like a stock. Commission fees apply ask your broker for what these fees are. Past performances do not indicate or guarantee future success. As with any investment strategy, there is a possibility of profitability as well as loss. There is no assurance that the investment process will consistently lead to successful investing. Asset allocation and diversification do not eliminate the risk of experiencing investment losses.

DEDICATIONS

To my loving wife who was patient with me while I shut myself away in my office.

To my dearest friend Andrew Riley who gave me the push to write this book.

CONTENTS

WHO THIS BOOK IS FOR

When I set out to write this book, I had a very specific type of reader in mind. I wanted to share my valuable discovery of a pattern that reliably eliminates the risk in the markets, a risk amplified enormously by increased volatility and the more frequent boom and bust cycles caused by Fed-induced bubbles in the economy. If you have had it with the craziness of the violent ups and downs in the markets and seeing your portfolio shrink by as much as 40%-60% in a matter of weeks, this book is for you! I do not blame anyone who has given up on the markets or is about to throw in the towel, but do not despair because help is here!

I intend to change your investment results, as you have never thought possible, and I say this with complete confidence. The strategies that I will show you in this book were developed scientifically and they have been tested and proven in actual practice using my own money. I have seen the amazing investment results that can be enjoyed by applying my strategies, and now it is your turn to benefit from my discovery. You too can beat the market!

When writing this book, I designed it for those who already have at least a basic understanding of the various products and fundamentals of stock trading, who like to watch and maintain their own portfolio of investments. In cases where I mention something which may be unfamiliar to you, I assume that you should know about it. If this is not your case, I would recommend researching any such topic in more detail on the web (try www.investopedia.com or similar).

I am only interested in reaching people who are truly serious about making a difference in their investment results by applying a very effective proven method. For this reason, I have priced the book accordingly. If you could find a way to beat the S&P500 by as much as 100% or more, I have no doubt that you would consider the book worth much more than its price. Would you agree?

It is very important that you read this book completely and learn the trading system well, to ensure that you apply it in your own portfolio management successfully as intended. This book explains every recommended pattern in detail, so that you know and fully understand the strategies and are able to choose which part of the pattern to use.

Finally, a new edition of the book will be coming out at the beginning of every year with new data, adjustments to the strategies and possible new strategies, which you can use to diversify your portfolio and make sure your strategies are on track.

INTRODUCTION

You are encouraged to read this book in its entirety to understand the trading system revealed in its pages fully, before you attempt to apply the patterns in the management of your investment portfolio. Read it once, twice and three times if necessary, to learn it and know it like the back of your hand.

First off, the "buy & hold"' strategy is for chumps! Yeah, sure, over a long period of time, say decades, you will make money in the market investing this way. You can see this clearly on any chart of the popular indices like the S&P 500 or the Dow Jones Industrials, but try to convince people who had planned to retire back in 2008-2009. You will get plenty of hate from them! They saw the value of their pensions, 401Ks and IRAs drop 40% to 60% in a matter of months! They had worked hard for many years or decades putting away a good portion of their income to ensure a good life during their retirement years, and suddenly half of it was gone! In many cases, this meant having to postpone retirement, or at the very least, they had to accept a much lower retirement standard of living than planned.

Every time I see a market correction, the financial experts love to say that it is a great opportunity to add to your positions to take advantage of the sudden low prices. This is known in investment circles as the "average down" method. They always tell you not to panic, and instead they urge you to buy more shares and hold your position, because the market always rises and recovers over time. The question though is if all you had was $10,000 when you bought initially and held, and then a market correction occurs, how can you buy more stock when all your money is already in the market?

The approach presented in this book will not only protect you from sudden drops, but it will also show you how to take advantage of such drops to double your portfolio and over time outperform the S&P 500. The smart way to invest in these times of high volatility and market manipulations is to know when to exit the market to avoid the scary drops that drain your account and get back in at the lows before the inevitable recovery comes. Think of the difference that this makes! Think of the possibility of an earlier retirement and a much larger nest egg come retirement time! What a difference! This book will show exactly how to do this intelligently and safely.

You will no longer be a victim of large market drops when bubbles burst, or when big Wall Street players purposely move the markets up or down to make huge trading profits. You will not be as clueless sheep led to the slaughterhouse. Instead, you will be out of the market before the 20%-60% losses happen and back in at the lows to ride the market up, as the big Wall Street players pump it back up. The methods you will learn in this book will change everything!

In the following chapters, I will tell you the story of how the mistakes from my early investing days inspired me to go on a search for ways to improve my investment results. There was a strong determination to eliminate the unpleasant experiences of seeing large losses in my investments due to the market corrections. I found this to be unacceptable, and I was determined to put a stop to it. You will see detailed explanations of how I arrived at my successful trading system and a detailed analysis that will help you understand the pattern that is behind my breakthrough method. Finally, I will show you how to apply my system to your own investment portfolio to enable you to achieve the results that I have achieved with my investments.

GROWING PAINS

MUTUAL FUNDS

In my early investing days, I used mutual funds exclusively as my investment vehicle of choice, since it is much simpler and safer than individual stock picking, especially for beginners. For those of you who are not familiar with mutual funds, you can search the web for information beyond what I have covered here. You can find a typical general definition here:

http://www.investopedia.com/university/mutualfunds/mutualfunds.asp.

Some important facts you should know:

- Mutual funds are a collection of stocks and/or bonds for diversification purposes
- Professional managers manage these funds, so there are fees associated with investing in them
- There is a wide variety of mutual fund types available to the investor covering every industry sector, country, risk level, etc.

Each fund consists of a composite of companies selected by the fund manager based on their research, analysis and established allocation rules. Funds have specific rules governing the investment mix. Say, for example, an energy fund may be required to maintain a mix of 80% invested in oil companies and 20% in renewable energy (wind, solar).

Unfortunately, here is the kicker, supposing one of the companies selected by the fund manager was SolarCity (SCTY), and it goes up 100%, this is great, but the fund is now heavier in renewable energy than in oil and gas. The fund manager would then have to sell renewable energy companies to restore the mandated allocation ratio. He has some other companies in wind power but the fund must have a mix of solar and wind (another rule), so he sells some of the SolarCity stock to buy more oil companies. That restores the oil to renewable energy ratio back to the required 80:20. Now, if you have a stock that is performing that well, would you really want to sell it? In fact, SolarCity from its initial offering price has gone up 465%!

Because of the allocation rules put in place for mutual funds, fund managers are forced to make decisions to buy or sell to ensure the fund complies with the rules instead of enhancing returns for the investor. A trader would not do this when they have a stock that is performing so well! In a fund, there is always going to be one stock that outshines the others, and so this happens quite frequently!

Now suppose the opposite happened, oil was not doing well, and it started tanking. Well, guess what, that 80:20 ratio would be off again! The fund manager would have to reduce his exposure in renewable energy and buy more of the poorer performing oil stocks to maintain the ratio. This is kind of nuts! This is exactly the opposite of what a trader would do!

Due to the fees associated with mutual fund products, you cannot simply buy and sell them as done in trading. This type of product is designed for the "buy and hold" investment approach, which brings up another problem. Many years back, I had bought into five mutual funds, and I went on vacation backpacking around Europe. A week later, I went to an internet café to check my emails and while I was there, I thought I would also check on my funds. What a shock! Yikes! (That was a polite version of what I really thought...) My funds had dropped by 10 to 15% in a matter of a week! What happened? What could I have done to prevent this? There had to be a better way to invest than this.

FUNDAMENTAL INVESTING

I spent many years reading books on various trading strategies, from fundamental to technical and I found a few challenges with each of them.

For fundamental trading, I used trading platforms (like Ameritrade, eTrade) to find great companies using the following parameters to define my searches: PE ratios, EPS growth, market capitalization, price to sales, price to book, dividend yield, profit margin, return on equity and performance vs. industry. This approach is common for long term investing, but there is a challenge with picking stocks this way. Yes, you are picking stocks that have strong fundamentals, and in theory, they should do well over time, BUT does everyone else think the same? After all, the reality is that what moves stocks in the end is volume and not great fundamentals alone. Significant stock price moves require increasing volume (higher demand for the stock).

Investors do not always buy the stocks that technical traders buy, and technical trading is the source of most volume in the markets. You could be sitting on your nice stock with great fundamentals for years, and it might not move, because there is no demand for it! Something else to consider is that it might be a good company at the time you did your analysis, but will it still be good a year or two years from now? If not, you invested into a good company at the time, spent a few years watching it going nowhere, and then you pull out after giving up on it. That is dead money! You might as well put it in a money market account and at least you will make some money from interest without the risk of stocks!

Another lesson learned is that investing in individual companies is too risky. All it takes is a bad earnings report, a company not getting FDA approval for a drug, a rumor, etc., and traders will dump it causing a massive drop of 10%- 20% or more in value very quickly.

TECHNICAL TRADING

After giving up on fundamental analysis as an investing approach, I started looking into technical trading. To put it simply, this practice is purely about looking at charts and graphs, and letting the indicators make your trading decisions. This sounds reasonably solid, right? The next logical step was to find ways to minimize my risk, so I looked into buying into an industry sector or country portfolio and not into individual companies alone. However, I did not want to buy into mutual funds, since that was more suitable for a long-term buy and hold strategy.

Continuing my search for the perfect investment vehicle, I came across Exchanged Traded Funds (ETFs). With ETFs, I could invest in any sector and not take the high risk of investing in just a few companies. ETFs also have the advantage of stop loss orders to minimize my risk even further. This is because ETFs do not have the mutual fund disadvantage of fees. There is just the cost of brokerage commissions. For an excellent resource on ETFs, try this website: http://www.etf.com/etf-education-ce.html. There are many other resources on the web to help you select the right ETFs for you. I encourage you to do some research online to achieve a good command of the subject.

First I focused on looking at some of the best stock indices out there, the S&P500 and Dow Jones Industrial Average and later a few industry sector indices. Now I had several choices from a menu of trading vehicles. My approach was to do my technical analysis, wait for the bounce back and buy in. Then I would put my market stop loss order in to protect my capital and any profits. Here is the kicker, though. Despite having all the indicators pointing up, there was no guarantee that an indicator buy signal meant that the market had truly turned. In many cases, buy signals would be false, and the market would go in the opposite direction triggering my stop loss order.

I would lose out by a couple of percentage points in a matter of days, which is okay once, but if this happens a lot, those percentages start adding up! Adding insult to injury, once the stock had dropped and triggered my stop loss order, sometimes the stock would then rally back up missing my opportunity to make a profit. Then I would have to wait for it to hit resistance on the way up and come back down to the support line again, which could be a long time to wait without a profit.

I was also prone to emotions when deciding on my trades. Fear and greed would mess with my strategy logic or make me see indicators appear to be valid when they were just false positives. I needed something else to improve my winning odds.

My goal was to find a strategy that grew my portfolio far more aggressively than the S&P500, which had exposure to the same companies that make up the S&P500. It also had to take out the emotion factor (greed and fear) which can cause us to lose badly when we allow it. I wanted a solid reliable indication of when to buy and when to sell with lots of historical data to support it. I had embarked on my quest to find the holy grail of trading strategies.

FINDING THE PULSE OF THE MARKET

When I first started my search, I had one thing in mind, to find the pulse of the market. We all know that the market is volatile and bounces up or down from hearing it in the news every day. Was there a pattern one could use to predict accurately when a market turn is approaching? In chaos, there is order and I wanted to find that order.

If you look around, you will notice that there are many seemingly unpredictable things going on around us. We think that there is no predictability in our lives (that is the chaos), but if you pay close attention, there are patterns (the order) in everything. Let us start with the basics, day and night, winter, summer, holidays, Black Friday, Super Bowl, election years, Christmas, New Years, etc. These events are all patterns that can be used to predict certain human behaviors.

For example, during winter, it is colder and more gas and electricity are used. Taking a position in the energy sector could be a good idea. These are seasonally adjusted but what happens when it is a very bad winter? We use a lot more than estimated, hence when utility companies report their Q4 and Q1 earnings, they are higher than expected and boom, the utility company stock prices go up more than the seasonal adjustment.

During the Black Friday to Christmas period, we tend to buy more gifts, food, and alcohol than during the rest of the year. Take the Super Bowl game; just go to Costco one week before it and you will surely see the long lines of fans buying TVs in preparation for game day.

In fact, I bet that 90% of people do the exact same thing 90% of the time every week; drop off kids at school, go to work, have lunch at the same places, pick up kids, head home, make dinner, watch their favorite show, etc. I could go on and on about the things we do every year day in day out. Let us face it; humanity is very predictable just like clockwork, tick, tock, tick, tock, and that is what I wanted to tap.

With this in mind, I started thinking that there must be seasonal patterns in the various industries. Instead of trying to think about events and see if they have an impact, I decided to collect daily data on the S&P 500. Then I looked for patterns in the data. Later in this book, I cover other industry studies that outperform even this strategy.

When I found the first pattern, I wanted to dig deeper. My curiosity paid off, and I found more patterns, which were not seasonal. They were long-term cycles happening every 10 and 30 years. Initially, I was skeptical about my findings. After all, I was not looking at any other external factors like GDP, climate, currency exchanges, or demographics, which logic tells us should have an impact. However, the patterns kept repeating year after year.

Although the patterns found in this book are based on historical data, peaks and troughs can come earlier or later than predicated. In the next chapter, I will show you how protect yourself from this variability.

PROTECTING YOUR POSITIONS

Learn from my $30,000 mistake! When you lose that much money, the incentive to find a better way to invest is powerful. It surely moved me to put my brain in gear and let those brain cells work harder to keep me away from the poor house. You do not have to learn the hard way. Follow the recommendations on this page, and you will not lose your shirt.

As mentioned earlier, one of the problems with mutual funds is that you cannot put a stop loss order on them, so you are taking open-ended risks, and you are at the mercy of the seemingly unpredictable corrections and possibly crashes. You would have to watch them daily just in case a correction starts, and even in that case, it would probably happen so quickly, that a good portion of any gains you have would be lost.

With ETFs, it is different. You can buy in and immediately put a stop loss order in to protect yourself from big market corrections. The four trades (per year) strategy covered in this book relies on using the ETF products and placing stop losses orders to work properly.

As soon as you enter a position in one of the S&P 500 ETFs (and there are many out there), always place a stop loss order on it. If the correction comes earlier than predicted, the stop loss order will automatically get you out of the position before the market goes even lower. If the week to sell (per the method in this book) arrives, and you are still in the position, just cancel your stop loss order and sell the position at market.

WHAT IS A STOP ORDER?

A stop order, also as known as a stop-loss order, is an order you put in to sell stock that you already own. If the price hits a certain value, known as the stop price, it will execute the sale. When these orders are created they are not executed straight away but are then waiting for a condition to be met and depending on what you choose can be open for a specified time or when the stop price is hit. Once hit the order is executed and the stock is sold.

The great thing about these are you don't have to be sitting in front of the monitor watching your stocks once set that is it and then from time to time can be adjusted.

A stop order can be set in three ways. Effective for the day, which means it's only active for that day if it's not triggered during that time the order is simply cancelled. GTC (Good Till Cancelled) this still has an expiry date but it is usually out 2-3 months and can be extend too, this helps you not have to set a stop loss every day and is only triggered or cancelled upon request. Note that GTC are in conjunction with stop orders and are only triggered during an open market.

Lastly GTC EXT (Good Till Cancelled extended hours) same as GTC but can be triggered outside market hours, this type can only be used on limit type orders.

TYPES OF STOP LOSSES

There are three types of stop orders

- Market Stop
- Stop limit
- Percentage or trailing stop

Market stop can only be set with an order price below the current market price. Once the market price falls and hits that order price it will change to a market order and execute. If there is high volatility in the market then the sell price maybe lower or higher than the price you set it to. Since it is a market stop order it can only be triggered when the market is open and trading and if the market opens way below your order price then the order will be triggered and sell at the price it opens at. This can be a problem if it triggers and then the market sudden rallies see figure 1.

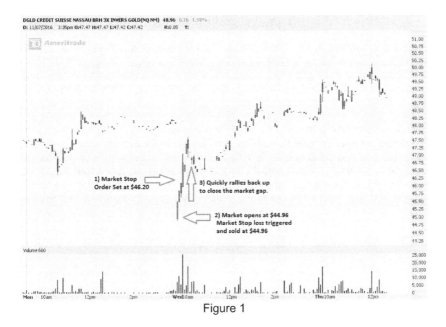

DGLD CREDIT SUISSE NASSAU BRH 3X INVERS GOLD(NQ NM) 48.96 0.76 1.59%
D: 11/07/2016 3:35pm O:47.47 H:47.47 L:47.42 C:47.42   R:0.05 Y:

Ameritrade

1) Market Stop
Order Set at $46.20

3) Quickly rallies back up
to close the market gap.

2) Market opens at $44.96
Market Stop loss triggered
and sold at $44.96

Volume 600

Figure 1

Stop limit order is similar to a stop market order except that the market price must hit the limit order price to be triggered. So in the example we had in figure 1. Where the market stop order was triggered because it was below the order price, in a limit order it would not have been triggered. Now this has its own pros and cons say that it then started to rally and get close to your stop order limit if it reaches it then it will then be triggered. However if it continued to fall then your stop loss has not done its job in protecting you.

I personally have gone with market stop losses for this reason, but you might want to do a stop limit order instead. Another thing that is different is that you can use GTC EXT, which means that in the hours before and after the market is open your stop limit order can be triggered if the price is hit.

Percent or trailing stop automatically adjusts its trigger price based on a percentage you define, for example say you set a percentage stop loss of 2%. Then the order will calculate the trigger price based on the current price minus the 2% of the value. As the current price continues to rise so does the trigger price minus 2% of the value. Now if the market price starts pulling back then trigger price stays the same if the market price falls down to the trigger price then the stop loss is executed.

It sounds great but the tricky part is determining that percentage, too tight and you could lose out on potential gains, as the market price naturally fluctuates as it goes up. Too lose and you could make profit but of small margins.

Since the strategies in this book are yearly, I recommend pulling a 1 or 2 year range chart and drawing a support and resistance channel. In figure 2 below, I have included an example of a price channel drawn on a chart with the stop loss order set below the support. The stop loss can either be a limit or market stop loss.

If you decide to use a trailing stop loss then you can use the same method and that would be your natural fluctuation. Say for example the difference between the resistance and support lines is 10% then your trailing stop loss should be set at 12-14%. However be warned if you are purchasing the stock and it's at the bottom of the support you might want to put a limit stop order much closer to the support first and then once the stock start to rally bullish change it to a trailing stop.

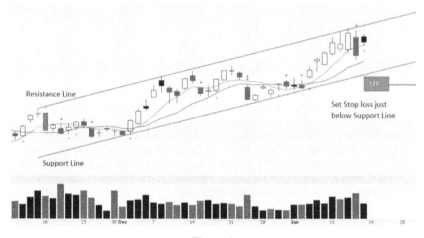

Figure 2

FINDING A METHOD THAT WORKS FOR YOU

Whatever order you decide to use make sure you consistently apply them. They are not just for preventing losses but also to lock in gains.

RULES TO REMEMBER

Here are some rules to remember and follow

1) Whenever you buy into a position put a stop loss on immediately! Get in the habit of doing this on all trades and check from time to time to make sure your stop losses have not expired.
2) Double check your stop order before committing. When I was new to trading I would sometimes not set the type of order and actually sell upon execution. Which means buying back in straight away occurring unnecessary transactional fees.

3) Make sure if you plan on selling all the stock to put the correct quantity.
4) If you buy more of a particular stock into a position don't forget to update your stop loss also with the correct quantity also.
5) Tighten up your stop loss when you see resistance. When you start seeing resistance you can just sell or tighten up your stop loss in case it changes direction. However, your stock can breakthrough this resistance so make sure the stop loss gives the stock room to bounce a little in case it does breakthrough.
6) **Always Always ALWAYS put a stop loss!** It's the difference of losing 30-50% instead of 5-10%

Here is what could be your trading strategy if you don't use a stop loss.

Figure 3.

THE ANALYSIS

In this chapter, I include a summary of the analysis that led to my discovery of the patterns associated with the trading system presented in this book. The analysis below proves that the pattern works, and I have also included the calculations (tables) that back up the resulting conclusions. Reading this chapter will satisfy your scientific curiosity, if you are so inclined. In any case, this is the evidence that proves the validity of my discovery, and it makes for some interesting reading, in addition to removing any doubt that the trading system does improve investment results dramatically.

AVERAGE MONTHLY RETURNS FROM 1982 TO 2017

The first step in my analysis was to gather a large amount of historical daily data on the S&P 500 to determine if there was seasonality in it. Using the data, I calculated the average monthly returns for each month of the year using data covering the period from 1980 to 2017. Table 1 below shows the results:

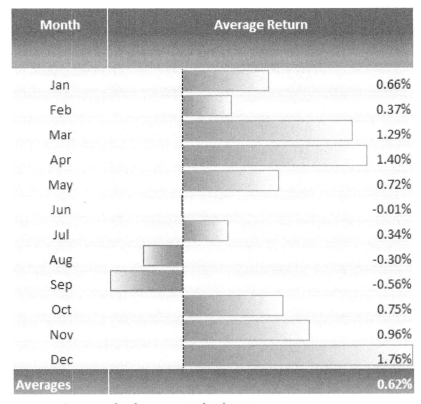

Month	Average Return
Jan	0.66%
Feb	0.37%
Mar	1.29%
Apr	1.40%
May	0.72%
Jun	-0.01%
Jul	0.34%
Aug	-0.30%
Sep	-0.56%
Oct	0.75%
Nov	0.96%
Dec	1.76%
Averages	0.62%

Figures from: 01/03/1983 to: 12/28/2017

Table 1

Bam! There it was! The power of math is truly amazing. I had finally found the pulse of the market for the S&P 500. August and September were the two months out of the year, on average, when the market corrects. It is not a time to be in a position in the S&P 500. This was a very significant finding narrowing down the time frame of highest risk in the market, but I wanted to be more precise than this. Was it at the start, middle, or the end of the month that I had to be out of the market to avoid losses?

The next step would be to look at weekly returns to get results that are more granular. This would make a difference, since a month or longer time frame was too wide a range for the selecting trade dates to keep me out of the market during corrections. There was too much risk of missing the market turns without greater granularity. Due to how fast markets move at the start of corrections, missing the market turns by just a few days would make the difference between success and failure in achieving the results that I was pursuing.

AVERAGE WEEKLY RETURNS FROM 1982 TO 2017

I started looking at weekly returns, but initial results were inconclusive. One week would be positive and another week would be negative, and I did not want a model that kept buying in and selling out every couple of weeks. I was looking to replace the buy and hold method with a smart trading system, but I did not want to end up with something that would be a bad case of 'churning' in my investment account. I was only interested in identifying the right time to enter or exit the market more precisely within this August - September time frame to more accurately time the market. This would maximize returns, which was my ultimate goal.

To get there, I set up a 'what if' analysis to figure out the weekly returns over a long period, and I adjusted the weeks that I traded to optimize the overall return. My analysis yielded weeks 19, 21, 36 and 42 as the ones to trade in order to get optimum results for the majority of years. Table 2 below shows the average weekly returns with the recommended action to take, buy or sell.

Week No.	BUY	SELL	Buy & Hold
1	0.17%		0.17%
2	-0.30%		-0.30%
3	0.27%		0.27%
4	-0.18%		-0.18%
5	0.67%		0.67%
6	0.17%		0.17%
7	0.36%		0.36%
8	-0.18%		-0.18%
9	0.05%		0.05%
10	0.47%		0.47%
11	0.43%		0.43%
12	0.54%		0.54%
13	-0.10%		-0.10%
14	0.27%		0.27%
15	0.29%		0.29%
16	0.36%		0.36%
17	0.65%		0.65%
18	0.60%		0.60%
19		-0.27%	-0.27%
20		-0.26%	-0.26%
21	-0.29%		-0.29%
22	0.59%		0.59%
23	0.20%		0.20%
24	0.02%		0.02%
25	0.25%		0.25%
26	-0.06%		-0.06%
27	0.26%		0.26%

Week No.	BUY	SELL	Buy & Hold
27	0.26%		0.26%
28	0.22%		0.22%
29	0.16%		0.16%
30	0.30%		0.30%
31	0.11%		0.11%
32	-0.22%		-0.22%
33	-0.01%		-0.01%
34	0.12%		0.12%
35	0.05%		0.05%
36		-0.03%	-0.03%
37		-0.09%	-0.09%
38	0.07%		0.07%
39		-0.36%	-0.36%
40	0.21%		0.21%
41		-0.28%	-0.28%
42	-0.08%		-0.08%
43	-0.06%		-0.06%
44	1.61%		1.61%
45	0.05%		0.05%
46	0.03%		0.03%
47	0.23%		0.23%
48	0.45%		0.45%
49	0.61%		0.61%
50	-0.38%		-0.38%
51	0.61%		0.61%
52	0.50%		0.50%
53	-0.02%		-0.02%
Averages	0.22%	-0.13%	0.17%

Figures from: 12/31/1982 to: 12/28/2017

Table 2

The 'Buy & Hold' column shows the investment results for each week of the year, and at the bottom of the column, I show the calculated weekly average for the year resulting from the 'Buy and Hold' strategy. You can see that the weekly average return for the year is 0.17%. By simply changing from buy and hold to a four trades per year approach by buying in weeks 21 and 42 and selling in weeks 19 and 36, results change dramatically for the better. Notice that the 'Buy' column shows a weekly average return of 0.22%, and the 'Sell' column shows a weekly average return of -0.13%. Clearly, by introducing the two sell trades, you avoid the -0.13% weekly average loss for those weeks.

Now that does not sound like much on the surface, but let us say you had $10,000 invested at the start of the year. Using the buy and hold method, if you bought and held for the entire year, at the end of the year you would have an average gain of 9.04% (i.e. $904) based on a 0.17% average weekly return. If instead, you made the four recommended trades, you would have an average gain of 11.86% (i.e. $1,186) based on a 0.22% average weekly return.

Applying the calculations to the entire analysis period (1983 to 2017), we can see the dramatic difference over a longer timeframe. If you had invested $10,000 in 1983 following the buy and hold method, your return would have been 1810% giving you a total market value of $191,094 by Dec 2017. That is not too shabby,

I think. However, if you had invested the $10,000 in 1983 and followed the four trades a year method (weeks, 19, 21, 36 and 42), your return would have been 2771% giving you a market value of $287,124 by Dec 2016. That is $100,000 more then buy and hold strategy! See Table 3 below for a visual summary of the comparison.

	Buy and Hold	Four Trades per Year
Average yearly return	$904 (9.04%)	$1186 (11.86%)
Total return for 1983-2017	$191,094 (1810%)	$287,124 (2771%)

Table 3

THE CORRECTION YEARS

From time to time, we know that major corrections happen in the markets, and when they do, they come fast and hit hard. What is fascinating about them is that they seem to happen in 10-11 year intervals. Also very interesting is that they happen during roughly the same timeframe in the year of the event.

Table 4 below shows monthly market returns from 1983 to 2017. If look at the years with the big dips (cells highlighted in red), do you see a pattern? Notice that the years 1987, 1998 and 2008 all had big corrections, and they all happened in the August – October timeframe.

Year	Jan	Feb	Mar	Apr	May	Jun	Jul	Aug	Sep	Oct	Nov	Dec
1983	5.0%	3.6%	1.4%	7.5%	0.2%	3.1%	-3.6%	1.5%	1.1%	-1.4%	1.7%	-0.9%
1984	-0.4%	-3.5%	0.6%	1.3%	-6.9%	0.0%	-1.7%	8.2%	0.7%	0.9%	-2.3%	2.7%
1985	8.6%	1.4%	-1.4%	-0.8%	6.3%	1.3%	-0.8%	-1.8%	-3.1%	2.6%	5.6%	5.4%
1986	1.0%	6.1%	6.0%	0.2%	5.2%	2.4%	-6.3%	7.7%	-6.9%	4.4%	1.4%	-2.8%
1987	11.2%	2.8%	3.1%	-1.4%	0.7%	4.9%	5.2%	3.9%	-0.5%	-23.1%	-10.0%	6.5%
1988	0.4%	5.0%	-3.1%	2.1%	0.2%	2.6%	0.1%	-3.9%	5.3%	2.8%	-1.9%	1.9%
1989	8.1%	-2.8%	2.7%	4.5%	3.7%	-1.2%	8.4%	2.2%	-1.3%	-3.0%	1.4%	0.8%
1990	-8.5%	0.9%	2.2%	-2.3%	8.7%	-1.4%	-0.9%	-9.3%	-5.3%	-3.5%	5.0%	1.9%
1991	5.4%	7.0%	1.3%	1.1%	2.5%	-4.4%	2.6%	2.2%	-1.1%	0.8%	-4.1%	9.4%
1992	-2.0%	0.8%	-2.1%	2.7%	0.7%	-2.2%	2.7%	-2.6%	0.4%	0.6%	2.0%	1.1%
1993	0.8%	0.2%	2.2%	-2.3%	1.8%	-0.7%	-0.2%	3.0%	-0.9%	1.4%	-1.6%	1.0%
1994	3.5%	-2.6%	-4.0%	2.7%	0.8%	-2.9%	2.7%	3.1%	-2.2%	2.3%	-3.1%	2.3%
1995	2.5%	3.6%	3.1%	2.6%	3.7%	2.1%	2.7%	0.4%	3.7%	0.0%	3.6%	1.5%
1996	2.5%	0.3%	0.2%	0.1%	2.2%	0.4%	-5.3%	0.3%	5.0%	2.4%	7.6%	-2.1%
1997	6.7%	0.5%	-4.8%	5.5%	6.2%	4.6%	7.1%	-5.0%	2.1%	-4.3%	1.8%	-0.5%
1998	0.5%	4.8%	5.2%	0.3%	-2.7%	3.9%	-2.4%	-14.0%	2.3%	11.4%	4.7%	4.6%
1999	4.2%	-2.7%	4.1%	3.2%	-3.9%	6.1%	-3.8%	-0.6%	-3.6%	6.3%	2.6%	5.1%
2000	-4.2%	-3.0%	8.7%	-3.6%	-3.3%	0.4%	-2.6%	5.5%	-5.5%	-0.5%	-7.5%	0.4%
2001	6.5%	-9.7%	-6.5%	9.0%	-0.8%	-2.9%	-2.1%	-6.8%	-8.1%	2.0%	5.1%	1.6%
2002	-2.1%	-1.4%	1.4%	-6.1%	-1.8%	-4.9%	-5.9%	3.6%	-7.2%	4.5%	3.9%	-5.9%
2003	-5.9%	-2.2%	1.6%	6.8%	5.2%	0.8%	0.8%	2.8%	-2.6%	3.2%	-0.1%	3.9%
2004	2.0%	0.9%	-2.6%	-2.2%	0.3%	1.8%	-2.4%	-0.2%	0.8%	-0.1%	3.8%	1.7%
2005	-1.7%	1.2%	-2.5%	-1.4%	2.5%	-0.9%	3.3%	-1.2%	0.6%	-1.6%	3.9%	-1.3%
2006	0.9%	-0.1%	0.3%	1.0%	-2.7%	-1.2%	-0.3%	2.6%	1.9%	3.5%	2.4%	1.6%
2007	1.5%	-2.7%	1.3%	4.1%	3.0%	-2.2%	-4.2%	0.6%	2.5%	0.2%	-1.8%	-0.3%
2008	-4.7%	-4.6%	-0.7%	1.1%	-0.6%	-7.6%	-1.4%	1.8%	-8.7%	-16.6%	-7.3%	10.7%
2009	-11.4%	-11.0%	13.9%	7.6%	4.7%	-2.5%	7.0%	1.8%	5.9%	0.6%	5.1%	0.6%
2010	-5.2%	1.4%	4.8%	0.7%	-9.4%	-3.7%	7.2%	-6.8%	5.6%	3.2%	-0.3%	4.3%
2011	1.1%	1.5%	1.5%	2.3%	-1.2%	0.5%	-3.5%	-5.3%	-6.1%	14.0%	2.4%	1.1%
2012	2.8%	3.1%	2.5%	-1.5%	-6.8%	6.6%	1.0%	2.3%	2.5%	-2.2%	-0.8%	1.2%
2013	2.4%	0.1%	3.4%	2.3%	3.0%	-2.1%	4.4%	-4.3%	2.6%	3.6%	2.5%	2.6%
2014	-2.7%	6.8%	1.4%	-0.1%	2.1%	1.8%	-2.2%	4.1%	-1.5%	3.7%	2.5%	0.3%
2015	-3.1%	4.1%	-2.3%	1.3%	0.0%	-2.3%	1.3%	-6.0%	0.3%	8.1%	-1.1%	-2.8%
2016	-3.6%	-0.4%	4.1%	-0.4%	0.8%	0.0%	3.4%	0.0%	-0.1%	-1.6%	4.1%	2.2%
2017	0.9%	3.7%	-1.4%	1.1%	1.0%	-0.3%	1.7%	-0.2%	1.7%	1.8%	2.6%	1.7%
Averages	0.7%	0.4%	1.3%	1.4%	0.7%	0.0%	0.3%	-0.3%	-0.6%	0.8%	1.0%	1.8%

Table 4

Looking at these years specifically, I wanted to see if the weeks 19, 21, 36, and 42 model was still supported or whether a different pattern was associated with large correction years requiring the introduction of another model for these years.

AVERAGE RETURNS FOR 1987, 1998 AND 2008

Once again, I did a 'what if' analysis to determine if a second model was necessary for the years 1987, 1998 and 2008. Table 5 below shows the results of my analysis.

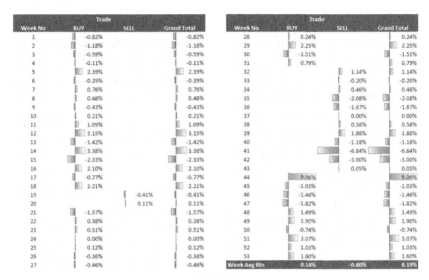

Week No	Trade BUY	SELL	Grand Total		Week No	Trade BUY	SELL	Grand Total
1	-0.82%		-0.82%		28	0.24%		0.24%
2	-1.18%		-1.18%		29	2.25%		2.25%
3	-0.59%		-0.59%		30	-1.51%		-1.51%
4	-0.11%		-0.11%		31	0.79%		0.79%
5	2.39%		2.39%		32		1.14%	1.14%
6	-0.39%		-0.39%		33		-0.20%	-0.20%
7	0.76%		0.76%		34		0.46%	0.46%
8	0.48%		0.48%		35		-2.08%	-2.08%
9	-0.43%		-0.43%		36		-1.67%	-1.67%
10	0.21%		0.21%		37		0.00%	0.00%
11	1.09%		1.09%		38		0.58%	0.58%
12	3.15%		3.15%		39		1.88%	1.88%
13	-1.42%		-1.42%		40		-1.18%	-1.18%
14	3.38%		3.38%		41		-6.84%	-6.84%
15	-2.33%		-2.33%		42		-3.00%	-3.00%
16	2.10%		2.10%		43		0.05%	0.05%
17	-0.77%		-0.77%		44	9.06%		9.06%
18	2.21%		2.21%		45	-1.03%		-1.03%
19		-0.41%	-0.41%		46	-1.46%		-1.46%
20		0.11%	0.11%		47	-1.82%		-1.82%
21	-1.57%		-1.57%		48	1.49%		1.49%
22	0.38%		0.38%		49	1.90%		1.90%
23	0.51%		0.51%		50	-0.74%		-0.74%
24	0.00%		0.00%		51	3.07%		3.07%
25	0.12%		0.12%		52	1.03%		1.03%
26	-0.36%		-0.36%		53	1.60%		1.60%
27	-0.46%		-0.46%		Week Avg Rtn	0.54%	-0.80%	0.19%

Table 5

For the large corrections years, I uncovered an even more dramatic set of figures. In this case, the 'Buy & Hold' strategy came in with an average weekly return of 0.19%. On the other hand, the four trades per year strategy (buy during weeks 21 & 44 and sell during weeks 19 & 32) yielded an average weekly return of 0.54%.

So let us say that at the beginning of January, you had $10,000 and you bought and held until Dec 31st. Your average weekly return would have been 0.19%, and your investment would have grown to $11,016, a profit of $1,016 (10% return).

Now, let us consider the case of the four trades per year. If instead of buying and holding until the end of the year, you had bought at the beginning of January with $10,000, sold in week 19, bought again in week 21, sold again in week 32 and finally bought back in week 44, you would have had an average weekly return of 0.54%. This approach would have yielded a net amount of $13,160, a profit of $3,160 (31.6% return). This is huge!

Why are the trade weeks different during years with large corrections? Well, quite simply big corrections take longer to play out, so the periods of being in cash are longer, and the recoveries from these corrections are large too. This translates to larger gains during the times when you are in the market following the end of the large corrections. Keep this difference in mind, since these trade weeks are only applicable to years ending in 7 and 8.

AVERAGE YEARLY RETURNS

Table 6 below shows the S&P500 returns going back as far as 1871. Across the top are the decades and the 'Years Ending' column represents the last digit of individual years within each decade. For example, row '4' contains years 1874, 1884, 1894, etc. Table cells are color coded to show the worst and best returns to help identify any patterns.

Average Annual Returns															
Year Ending	1870	1880	1890	1900	1910	1920	1930	1940	1950	1960	1970	1980	1990	2000	2010
0		27%	-6%	21%	-3%	-14%	-23%	-9%	34%	-1%	4%	33%	-3%	-9%	15%
1	16%	0%	19%	19%	4%	10%	-44%	-9%	23%	29%	15%	-5%	31%	-12%	2%
2	11%	4%	6%	8%	7%	29%	-6%	22%	18%	-9%	19%	21%	8%	-22%	16%
3	-2%	-5%	-19%	-17%	-5%	5%	57%	24%	-1%	23%	-15%	23%	10%	29%	32%
4	5%	-12%	4%	32%	-5%	27%	-8%	20%	56%	17%	-27%	6%	1%	11%	14%
5	5%	30%	5%	21%	31%	26%	55%	39%	28%	12%	38%	32%	38%	5%	1%
6	-14%	12%	3%	1%	8%	12%	33%	-12%	6%	-10%	24%	19%	23%	16%	10%
7	-1%	-1%	20%	-24%	-19%	37%	-32%	3%	-9%	24%	-8%	6%	34%	5%	20%
8	16%	3%	29%	39%	18%	48%	18%	10%	43%	11%	6%	17%	29%	-37%	
9	49%	7%	4%	16%	20%	-9%	3%	16%	12%	-9%	19%	32%	21%	27%	
Avg Yearly Rtn.	9%	6%	7%	12%	6%	17%	5%	10%	21%	9%	8%	18%	19%	1%	14%

Table 6

In Table 7 below, under the 'Average last:' column grouping, I took the average of each 'Year Ending' in 0 through 9 going back to 1920 (100 years), 1970 (50 years) and 1990 (30 years).

18

Year Ending	Average last: 100 years	Average last: 50 years	Average last: 30 Years
0	3%	8%	1%
1	4%	6%	7%
2	10%	8%	0%
3	19%	16%	24%
4	12%	1%	9%
5	28%	23%	15%
6	12%	18%	16%
7	8%	11%	20%
8	16%	4%	-4%
9	12%	25%	24%
Average Return	12%	12%	11%

Table 7

Analysis of the data above yields the following conclusions:

1. Looking at 100, 50 and 30-year averages they show consistent trending. I was speculating that perhaps the 30-year averages would be vastly different from the 100-year averages, due to changes in population, industry, technology, etc. However, that does not seem to be the case.
2. Any years ending in 0 generally tend to have the weakest returns out of all the other years.
3. Years ending in 7 & 8 do show very strong returns every 30-40 years (1897 & 1898, 1927 & 1928, 1958 & 1967 and 1997 & 1998 highlighted). Consequently, the next predicted strong gains are set for 2027 and 2028.
4. Strong consistent years to be in the S&P500 are years ending in 3, 5, 6 and 9.

THE S&P500 TRADING SYSTEM

Following all my painstaking analysis, testing my methodology with my own investments and carefully verifying the results of all my investigations, I had concluded my long search for a trading system far superior to the traditional buy and hold method.

Here is the complete four trades per year strategy for the S&P 500. Please, go through all the instructions below carefully to familiarize completely with the rules and exceptions. It is important to keep in mind that the pattern is not the same for all years. There are different patterns that apply to different year groupings due to the cyclical nature of the markets. Understanding the difference will help you prevent using the wrong pattern and getting the wrong results.

PATTERN 1 - ANNUAL

For all years, except ones that end with a 7 or 8 (i.e., 2015, 2016, 2019, 2020, etc.), trade as follows:

Week	Trade
19	SELL
21	BUY
36	SELL
42	BUY

Table 8

There are long market cycles identified in my analysis, which have an effect on market performance in addition to the rules covered above. The following trading rules compensate for these effects:

PATTERN 2 – EVERY 10 YEARS

Big corrections occur every 10 years on the years ending in 7 & 8. Based on this, the next big correction will occur during the year 2018. For the year 2018, use weeks 21 & 44 to buy and weeks 19 & 32 to sell (Table 9).

Week	Trade
19	SELL
21	BUY
32	SELL
44	BUY

Table 9

PATTERN 3 – EVERY 30 TO 40 YEARS

Years ending in 7 & 8 do show very strong returns every 30-40 years (1897 & 1898, 1927 & 1928, 1958 & 1967 and 1997 & 1998), and the next predicted strong gains are set for 2027 and 2028. For these years, use weeks 21 & 42 to buy and weeks 19 & 36 to sell (Table 8). If strong returns do not materialize in years 2027 and 2028, then expect that strong returns will happen in 2037 and 2038 instead. This pattern repeats every 30 or 40 years.

Note: It is always strongly recommended to have a stop loss order on all positions, just in case the dips and corrections come in a week or two earlier than predicted.

PATTERN 4 – EVERY DECADE

From Table 7 you can see certain years perform better than others. If you are planning to increase your exposure to the market, the years to do so are ones that end in 3, 5, 6 and 9. Poor performing years in the market are ones that end in 0, so avoid increasing your exposure in such years.

BUY & HOLD VS. THE FOUR TRADES SYSTEM COMPARISON

We have all heard the famous saying "a picture is worth a thousand words". So, what better way to demonstrate the difference that the four trades per year strategy makes over the old buy and hold method than using one? Figure 4 below illustrates the four trades per year strategy with the variation for years ending in 7 and 8. As you can see, over time this strategy outperforms the S&P 500 by 100% in 30 years.

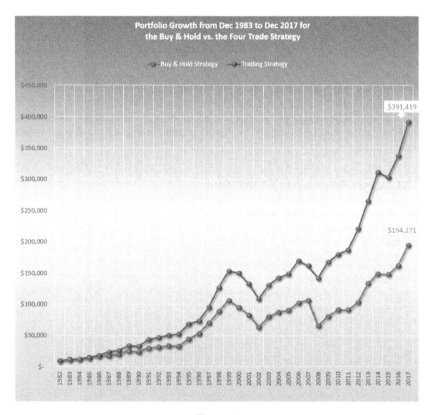

Figure 4

In Table 10 below, the win column in the adjacent table shows whether it outperformed the S&P 500 for each year in the range, which has a 64% success rate. This means that in some years, the four trades per year strategy will not perform, and in some cases, it did not outperform the S&P 500 for as long as three years straight. Do not be discouraged by this. If you stick with the strategy, I can assure you that it will outperform over time.

| Year | Market Value | | Annual Returns | | Win |
	Buy & Hold Strategy	Trading Strategy	Buy & Hold Strategy	Trading Strategy	
1982	$ 10,000	$ 10,000	0%	0%	Y
1983	$ 11,922	$ 11,285	19%	13%	N
1984	$ 12,089	$ 11,865	1%	5%	Y
1985	$ 15,273	$ 14,743	26%	24%	N
1986	$ 17,505	$ 18,309	15%	24%	Y
1987	$ 17,860	$ 24,031	2%	31%	Y
1988	$ 20,075	$ 26,362	12%	10%	N
1989	$ 25,546	$ 34,055	27%	29%	Y
1990	$ 23,870	$ 32,643	-7%	-4%	Y
1991	$ 30,150	$ 43,707	26%	34%	Y
1992	$ 31,496	$ 47,319	4%	8%	Y
1993	$ 33,718	$ 50,756	7%	7%	Y
1994	$ 33,199	$ 52,821	-2%	4%	Y
1995	$ 44,523	$ 68,457	34%	30%	N
1996	$ 53,545	$ 73,486	20%	7%	N
1997	$ 70,148	$ 94,876	31%	29%	N
1998	$ 88,856	$ 127,183	27%	34%	Y
1999	$ 106,206	$ 153,110	20%	20%	Y
2000	$ 95,437	$ 150,361	-10%	-2%	Y
2001	$ 82,990	$ 133,108	-13%	-11%	Y
2002	$ 63,598	$ 108,515	-23%	-18%	Y
2003	$ 80,376	$ 131,166	26%	21%	N
2004	$ 87,604	$ 142,625	9%	9%	N
2005	$ 90,233	$ 148,395	3%	4%	Y
2006	$ 102,523	$ 169,366	14%	14%	Y
2007	$ 106,141	$ 161,828	4%	-4%	N
2008	$ 65,292	$ 141,944	-38%	-12%	Y
2009	$ 80,606	$ 167,254	23%	18%	N
2010	$ 90,909	$ 180,095	13%	8%	N
2011	$ 90,906	$ 186,958	0%	4%	Y
2012	$ 103,093	$ 220,662	13%	18%	Y
2013	$ 133,610	$ 265,465	30%	20%	N
2014	$ 148,829	$ 311,331	11%	17%	Y
2015	$ 147,748	$ 303,003	-1%	-3%	N
2016	$ 161,835	$ 337,304	10%	11%	Y
2017	$ 194,271	$ 391,419	20%	16%	N
Averages	-	-	9.8%	11.5%	86.3%

Table 10

Table 11 below shows the actual trades associated with Figure 4 and Table 10 in detail. For each year, you can see the recommended trade action for each trade week, so you can see all the patterns together in one place.

23

Trade Action	SELL	BUY	SELL	SELL	BUY	BUY
Week Number	19	21	32	36	42	44
1983	5/2/1983	5/16/1983		8/29/1983	10/10/1983	
1984	5/7/1984	5/21/1984		9/4/1984	10/15/1984	
1985	5/6/1985	5/20/1985		9/3/1985	10/14/1985	
1986	5/5/1986	5/19/1986		9/2/1986	10/13/1986	
1987	5/4/1987	5/18/1987	8/3/1987			10/26/1987
1988	5/2/1988	5/16/1988	8/1/1988			10/24/1988
1989	5/8/1989	5/22/1989		9/5/1989	10/16/1989	
1990	5/7/1990	5/21/1990		9/4/1990	10/15/1990	
1991	5/6/1991	5/20/1991		9/3/1991	10/14/1991	
1992	5/4/1992	5/18/1992		8/31/1992	10/12/1992	
1993	5/3/1993	5/17/1993		8/30/1993	10/11/1993	
1994	5/2/1994	5/16/1994		8/29/1994	10/10/1994	
1995	5/8/1995	5/22/1995		9/5/1995	10/16/1995	
1996	5/6/1996	5/20/1996		9/3/1996	10/14/1996	
1997	5/5/1997	5/19/1997	8/4/1997			10/27/1997
1998	5/4/1998	5/18/1998	8/3/1998			10/26/1998
1999	5/3/1999	5/17/1999		8/30/1999	10/11/1999	
2000	5/1/2000	5/15/2000		8/28/2000	10/9/2000	
2001	5/7/2001	5/21/2001		9/4/2001	10/15/2001	
2002	5/6/2002	5/20/2002		9/3/2002	10/14/2002	
2003	5/5/2003	5/19/2003		9/2/2003	10/13/2003	
2004	5/3/2004	5/17/2004		8/30/2004	10/11/2004	
2005	5/2/2005	5/16/2005		8/29/2005	10/10/2005	
2006	5/8/2006	5/22/2006		9/5/2006	10/16/2006	
2007	5/7/2007	5/21/2007	8/6/2007			10/29/2007
2008	5/5/2008	5/19/2008	8/4/2008			10/27/2008
2009	5/4/2009	5/18/2009		8/31/2009	10/12/2009	
2010	5/3/2010	5/17/2010		8/30/2010	10/11/2010	
2011	5/2/2011	5/16/2011		8/29/2011	10/10/2011	
2012	5/7/2012	5/21/2012		9/4/2012	10/15/2012	

2013	5/6/2013	5/20/2013		9/3/2013	10/14/2013	
2014	5/5/2014	5/19/2014		9/2/2014	10/13/2014	
2015	5/4/2015	5/18/2015		8/31/2015	10/11/2015	

Table 11

Remember that trade weeks 19 and 21 apply to every year, but trade weeks 32 and 44 apply only for years ending in 7 & 8, and trade weeks 36 and 42 apply to all other years.

WHY IS THE FOUR TRADES SYSTEM SO EFFECTIVE?

I have no doubt that you have heard of compounding. We usually hear about it regarding the advantage of long-term savings accounts, 401K accounts, etc. Well, the power of compounding is the secret behind the enormous success of this trading system when compared with buy and hold. Every time you exit a position to avoid the dips, you are locking in your profits. Then, when it is time to buy again in a bullish market, you will be making new gains on the money you have rather than recovering back to where you were before the correction. Essentially, you are making money on money that you would have lost otherwise, had you stayed in the market during the correction.

Below is an illustration of the effectiveness of compounding. The buy & hold position value is going up and down as the S&P 500 index rises and falls, while the four trades system has you in a position only when the market is rising. As you can see in the comparison table below, near the last period, 10% of $194.87 is $19.49 and 10% of $129.28 is $12.93. Notice that the result from the four trades system is a gain of 114.36% that of the buy and hold method which is 42.21% in that last period.

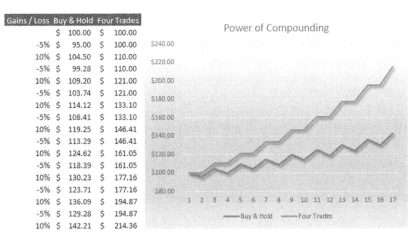

Gains / Loss	Buy & Hold	Four Trades
	$ 100.00	$ 100.00
-5%	$ 95.00	$ 100.00
10%	$ 104.50	$ 110.00
-5%	$ 99.28	$ 110.00
10%	$ 109.20	$ 121.00
-5%	$ 103.74	$ 121.00
10%	$ 114.12	$ 133.10
-5%	$ 108.41	$ 133.10
10%	$ 119.25	$ 146.41
-5%	$ 113.29	$ 146.41
10%	$ 124.62	$ 161.05
-5%	$ 118.39	$ 161.05
10%	$ 130.23	$ 177.16
-5%	$ 123.71	$ 177.16
10%	$ 136.09	$ 194.87
-5%	$ 129.28	$ 194.87
10%	$ 142.21	$ 214.36

Power of Compounding

FUTURE TRADING SCHEDULE

I have made it easier for you to use my trading method. Table 12 below contains all recommended trades for years 2016-2045. I have done all the work of looking through the tables and rules to figure out all the correct trades including the trade dates for the next 30 years.

The trade dates in the table are meant to be used as a **guide**. I have given the week beginning date in the table. You have a week to make the trade, so you can make the trade a few days before or after the date shown for each trade depending on what the market is doing. If it is still bullish, stay in a bit longer. If it is bearish, and the schedule recommends selling, then sell a few days earlier.

Sometimes, as was the case in 2015, my stop loss order kicked me out one week earlier on 8/20/2015 than my model recommended. Corrections may sometimes occur earlier or later, but during the ensuing recovery, the market takes the same amount of time to bounce back as always. Therefore, the next buy trade will likely come a week earlier than predicted. In this case, I changed my trade calendar from buying on 10/11/2015 to buying one week earlier than scheduled on 10/2/2015. If your stop loss is set just below the support, and it comes a week or two earlier, then set your calendar to buy in earlier retrospectively.

Trade Action	SELL	BUY	SELL	SELL	BUY	BUY
Week No.	19	21	32	36	42	44
2016	5/2/2016	5/16/2016		8/29/2016	10/10/2016	
2017	5/8/2017	5/22/2017	8/7/2017			10/30/2017
2018	5/7/2018	5/21/2018	8/6/2018			10/29/2018
2019	5/6/2019	5/20/2019		9/2/2019	10/14/2019	
2020	5/4/2020	5/18/2020		8/31/2020	10/12/2020	
2021	5/3/2021	5/17/2021		8/30/2021	10/11/2021	
2022	5/2/2022	5/16/2022		8/29/2022	10/10/2022	
2023	5/8/2023	5/22/2023		9/4/2023	10/16/2023	
2024	5/6/2024	5/20/2024		9/2/2024	10/14/2024	
2025	5/5/2025	5/19/2025		9/1/2025	10/13/2025	
2026	5/4/2026	5/18/2026		8/31/2026	10/12/2026	
2027	5/3/2027	5/17/2027		**8/30/2027**	**10/11/2027**	
2028	5/1/2028	5/15/2028		**8/28/2028**	**10/9/2028**	
2029	5/7/2029	5/21/2029		9/3/2029	10/15/2029	
2030	5/6/2030	5/20/2030		9/2/2030	10/14/2030	
2031	5/5/2031	5/19/2031		9/1/2031	10/13/2031	
2032	5/3/2032	5/17/2032		8/30/2032	10/11/2032	
2033	5/2/2033	5/16/2033		8/29/2033	10/10/2033	
2034	5/8/2034	5/22/2034		9/4/2034	10/16/2034	
2035	5/7/2035	5/21/2035		9/3/2035	10/15/2035	
2036	5/5/2036	5/19/2036		9/1/2036	10/13/2036	
2037	5/4/2037	5/18/2037	8/3/2037			10/26/2037
2038	5/3/2038	5/17/2038	8/2/2038			10/25/2038
2039	5/2/2039	5/16/2039		8/29/2039	10/10/2039	
2040	5/7/2040	5/21/2040		9/3/2040	10/15/2040	
2041	5/6/2041	5/20/2041		9/2/2041	10/14/2041	
2042	5/5/2042	5/19/2042		9/1/2042	10/13/2042	
2043	5/4/2043	5/18/2043		8/31/2043	10/12/2043	
2044	5/2/2044	5/16/2044		8/29/2044	10/10/2044	
2045	5/8/2045	5/22/2045		9/4/2045	10/16/2045	

Table 12

ABOUT YOU AS A TRADER

I have explained the details of the four trades per year strategy, and how it is far superior compared to the traditional buy and hold strategy. One thing to keep in mind, though, is that any investment strategy will be based on probabilities, so it is not 100% guaranteed as I showed in the conclusion chapter. It is possible, for example, that the four trades per year strategy sometimes does not outperform the S&P 500 for as long as three years straight. Now let us think about that for a moment. It can be very discouraging to execute the strategy faithfully for three years without getting the expected results.

Here is where the successful traders and the unsuccessful traders are distinguished. Unsuccessful traders are not patient, so they keep changing their strategy when they do not see results immediately. The funny thing is that as soon as they do, the disregarded old strategy starts outperforming, so they switch back. This frequent back and forth is what makes them unsuccessful. If you know that a strategy works, just give it time without letting the variations in performance over the years affect you your judgment.

Using an analogy, say you have a bag of marbles that represents the market and there is an equal number of blue and red marbles. This means that at the start you have a 50:50 chance of pulling out a red or a blue marble. Now suppose that you pull out a red marble on the first try, and on the second try, you pull out another red marble. According to the laws of statistics, every time you pull out a red marble, you are increasing your odds that you will pull out a blue marble next time. If you switch strategy, it is equivalent to starting over with a new bag of marbles, which explains why it is a bad idea to keep switching your strategies.

Successful trading requires discipline, and this means selecting a strategy that you are comfortable with and sticking with it, no matter the outcome at that present time.

WHAT COMES NEXT?

As amazingly accurate and reliable as this strategy is, we know that nothing remains unchanged over time. Market cycles and behaviors can change due to many factors beyond our control. These changes can occur due to changes in the political atmosphere, market psychology, economic policy, fiscal policy, Federal Reserve policy, etc. For this reason, I will continue my research to ensure that my strategy remains valid, as factors affecting the market change.

As my research uncovers impacts to market behavior and timing, I will tweak the S&P 500 trading strategy, so from time to time, I will make available new versions of this book. When a new version is released, it is highly likely that the strategy stated in this book may be outdated, so it will be **important to keep an eye out for new versions**. This will ensure that your trading results remain optimized.

Sign up and keep informed go to; http://www.discoveringthepattern.com/sign-up/

In the next few chapters, I will show you other strategies for specific industry sector ETFs that will produce results that are even more amazing. Adding these is a great way to diversify your portfolio. Since I explained already the analysis that I used to find the pattern in the S&P500, the following chapters will just show the data and the results as well as the percentage accuracy of each scenario.

OTHER ETF PATTERNS

When I started my analysis on other ETFs, my objective was to come up with a model yielding the best possible return with a high degree of accuracy. I looked at four factors when adjusting each model for optimal performance and accuracy. These factors where:

- Annual winning probability
- Monthly winning probability
- Total Return from the Buy & Hold method
- Total Return from the Trading Strategy

My analysis showed that in some cases for some ETFs, only two trades were needed per year, and in some cases, as many as six trades were needed per year. However, I do not usually go higher than six trades per year in any ETF model. As I mentioned earlier in the book, I did not want to build something that requires being constantly in and out of an ETF. Account churn usually benefits the broker only. In addition, if for the next year the market shifted by a week, losses could be larger than desired. I was only interested in finding the large swings in the year that happened consistently.

When I calculated which trades to use, I also tried to keep the winning probabilities as high as possible. For example, if I move the trading strategy to buy one week ahead, and it gives me an extra 20% return, but my winning probability goes from 80% down to 50%, then I would adjust the model back to an 80% winning probability and leave it at that. The compromise yields the optimum result, which is my objective.

In the following chapters, I present the analysis for each of several ETFs. Each chapter has the following content:

- Summary
- Monthly analysis table
- Weekly average returns table
- Historical yearly returns table and chart
- Trading instructions for the ETF

The summary section contains the following information:

- ETF name
- Ticker symbol
- Information website address
- Description
- Date range of the data that was used for the analysis (I always try to use as much daily data as possible in my analyses for best results)
- Metrics to help you determine risk vs. reward and if the ETF and trading strategy is right for you

- Monthly and annual winning probabilities are provided, to show the accuracy of the strategy
- Average annual returns for both buy & hold and trading strategy, so that you can see the difference in performance as well as the delta between the two returns
- A table containing the specific recommended trading weeks and buy or sell instructions for optimum returns

The Monthly Analysis table shows the average monthly returns for the buy & hold strategy vs. the trading strategy, the standard deviation of the monthly returns which indicates which months are more volatile than others and the winning monthly probability.

The Weekly Average Returns table shows the average weekly returns and the position based on the summary.

Historical yearly returns table shows the market values of buy and hold vs. trading strategy. These are based purely on the recommended trading weeks, and stop losses were not applied to the simulations. Also shown are the Annual Returns of the buy & hold vs. trading strategy and the annual wins and percentage of wins.

THE RESEARCHED ETF LIST

In some cases, the trading strategy works like a charm, and in other cases, it doesn't do so well. In these cases, a buy & hold strategy might actually be a better option along with a stop loss that is adjusted periodically to lock in gains when an out of the norm market correct occurs. You can easily spot the cases for which the trading strategy doesn't work by looking at the metrics. For these cases, the average annual returns are much smaller (less than a 1% difference compared to the buy and hold results). The reason for covering them in this book is to show you that I wanted to be non-biased. All industry sectors that I have researched are covered, so you know for which ones the trading strategy works well vs. for which ones it doesn't.

In my research, I also included some Inverse ETFs (short position ETFs). When the market is in a downturn, these are good trading vehicles for adding extra returns instead of just sitting on cash. Typically, these positions are held for a short time, a few weeks or so.

Table 13 below shows you a summary of all the ETFs I have researched. I have studied their average annual returns for buy & hold and trading strategies, the delta's and winning probabilities, for ease of comparison. This collection of trading vehicles gives you a diverse arsenal to use in your portfolio to increase your investment returns optimally.

Ticker	Name	Industry Sector	Position	Avg Annual Return		Delta	Winning Probability	
				Buy & Hold	Trading Strategy		Monthly	Annually
^GSPC	SP500	Index	long	9.9%	10.9%	1.1%	56.2%	85.5%
DIA	Dow Jones Industial Average	Index	long	8.8%	13.2%	4.4%	70.8%	61.9%
FTY	iShares Real Estate 50 ETF	Real Estate	long	8.4%	31.4%	23.0%	66.7%	63.6%
IYH	iShares U.S. Healthcare ETF	Healthcare	long	7.5%	8.1%	0.6%	90.7%	50.0%
IGM	iShares North American Tech ETF	Technology	long	10.0%	13.1%	3.1%	84.7%	72.2%
IYE	iShares U.S. Energy ETF	Energy	long	7.9%	13.1%	5.2%	73.5%	63.2%
IAU	iShares Gold Trust	Gold	long	8.8%	11.3%	2.5%	75.6%	78.6%
IYF	iShares U.S. Financials ETF	Finance	long	5.2%	10.4%	5.1%	77.4%	73.7%
IYJ	iShares U.S. Industrials ETF	Industrials	long	8.1%	9.8%	1.8%	90.5%	73.7%
IYT	iShares Transportation Average ETF	Industrials	long	11.7%	17.2%	5.6%	89.9%	66.7%
IYM	iShares U.S. Basic Materials ETF	Basic Materials	long	10.3%	14.6%	4.2%	85.3%	84.2%
IYW	iShares U.S. Technology ETF	Technology	long	6.1%	8.2%	2.1%	80.2%	73.7%
IYZ	iShares U.S. Telecommunications ETF	Telecommunications	long	0.6%	6.2%	5.6%	75.9%	68.4%
IDU	iShares U.S. Utilities ETF	Utilities	long	8.6%	9.3%	0.7%	71.6%	52.6%
IYR	iShares U.S. Real Estate ETF	Real Estate	long	11.1%	15.4%	4.3%	83.4%	57.9%
IYK	iShares U.S. Consumer Goods ETF	Consumer	long	8.8%	9.8%	1.0%	87.7%	63.2%
IYC	iShares U.S. Consumer Services ETF	Consumer	long	8.4%	10.8%	2.4%	81.0%	57.9%
GOLD	Randgold Resources Limited	Basic Materials	long	9.7%	12.5%	2.8%	87.8%	60.8%
DBB	PowerShares DB Base Metals ETF	Basic Materials	long	2.7%	13.1%	10.4%	79.5%	75.0%
AGQ	ProShares Ultra Silver	Basic Materials	long	9.6%	43.6%	34.0%	69.4%	81.8%
UPV	ProShares Ultra FTSE Europe	Equities - International	long	16.6%	29.4%	12.8%	75.0%	77.8%
EFO	ProShares Ultra MSCI EAFE	Equities - International	long	12.1%	24.3%	12.2%	81.6%	80.0%
EZJ	ProShares Ultra MSCI Japan	Equities - International	long	11.4%	22.2%	10.9%	84.5%	80.0%
XPP	ProShares Ultra FTSE China 50	Equities - International	long	7.6%	30.4%	22.8%	85.4%	90.0%
EET	ProShares Ultra MSCI Emerging Markets	Equities - International	long	11.1%	26.3%	15.2%	86.4%	80.0%
	High Risk High Return ETF's Below							
CURE	Direxion Daily Healthcare Bull 3X Shares	Healthcare	long	47.4%	60.2%	12.7%	94.9%	87.5%
SPXL	Direxion Daily S&P500® Bull 3X Shares	SP500	long	38.6%	52.4%	13.7%	91.7%	70.0%
SPXS	Direxion Daily S&P500® Bear 3X Shares	SP500	short	-42.5%	-1.9%	40.6%	78.7%	100.0%
ERX	Daily Energy Bull 3x Shares	Energy	long	5.4%	30.5%	25.2%	87.0%	80.0%
ERY	Daily Energy Bear 3x Shares	Energy	short	-30.9%	8.6%	39.5%	69.4%	90.0%
TECL	Daily Technology Bull 3x Shares	Technology	long	58.2%	78.6%	20.4%	85.2%	60.0%
TECS	Daily Technology Bear 3x Shares	Technology	short	-48.0%	6.6%	54.6%	69.4%	100.0%
FAS	Direxion Daily Financial Bull 3X Shares	Finance	long	26.7%	39.4%	12.8%	92.7%	70.0%
FAZ	Direxion Daily Financial Bear 3X Shares	Finance	short	-48.1%	3.1%	51.2%	66.7%	100.0%
DRN	Daily Real Estate Bull 3x Shares	Real Estate	long	41.5%	81.4%	40.0%	84.3%	70.0%
DRV	Daily Real Estate Bear 3x Shares	Real Estate	short	-45.1%	14.3%	59.4%	70.6%	100.0%
RETL	Daily Retail Bull 3x Shares	Retail	long	42.9%	57.1%	14.2%	87.8%	88.9%
NUGT	Direxion Daily Gold Miners Bull 3X ETF	Basic Materials	long	-42.7%	36.2%	78.9%	70.2%	87.5%
DUST	Direxion Daily Gold Miners Bear 3X ETF	Basic Materials	short	-1.6%	44.7%	46.3%	92.9%	100.0%
UCC	ProShares Ultra Consumer Services	Consumer	long	16.2%	33.2%	17.0%	84.7%	75.0%
^VIX	VOLATILITY S&P 500 (^VIX)	Index	long	3.5%	40.3%	36.7%	66.4%	86.2%

Table 13

32

DOW JONES INDUSTRIAL AVERAGE ETF (DIA)

SUMMARY

Ticker: DIA

Description: The investment seeks to provide investment results that, before expenses, correspond generally to the price and yield performance of the Dow Jones Industrial Average (the "DJIA"). The Trust seeks to achieve its investment objective by holding a portfolio of the common stocks that are included in the DJIA (the "Portfolio"), with the weight of each stock in the Portfolio substantially corresponding to the weight of such stock in the DJIA.

Data From: 01/20/1998 To: 12/28/2017		Total Return	
Winning Probability		Buy & Hold:	385.03%
• Monthly:	70.83%	Trading Strategy:	1,024.58%
• Annually:	61.90%	Trading Weeks:	
		BUY	**SELL**
Average Annual Returns		10	3
• Buy & Hold:	8.99%		
• Trading Strategy:	13.19%	27	19
• Delta:	4.2%	40	31

MONTHLY ANALYSIS

Month	Average Return Buy & Hold Strategy	Average Return Trading Strategy	Standard Dev of Month Return (Volatility)	Percentage Wins
Jan	-1.51%	-0.15%	3.62%	60.00%
Feb	0.19%	0.12%	4.33%	35.00%
Mar	1.80%	1.90%	4.03%	95.00%
Apr	2.01%	2.01%	3.85%	100.00%
May	-0.55%	0.25%	3.53%	60.00%
Jun	-0.85%	0.27%	3.30%	65.00%
Jul	0.47%	0.68%	3.44%	50.00%
Aug	-0.68%	0.00%	4.74%	35.00%
Sep	-0.99%	-0.28%	4.49%	50.00%
Oct	2.45%	2.45%	5.66%	100.00%
Nov	2.09%	2.09%	3.35%	100.00%
Dec	1.58%	1.63%	2.89%	100.00%
Averages	0.50%	0.91%	4.14%	70.83%

Figures from: 12/31/1997 to: 12/28/2017

WEEKLY AVERAGE RETURNS

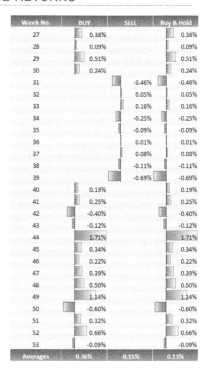

Week No.	BUY	SELL	Buy & Hold
1	0.12%		0.12%
2	-0.21%		-0.21%
3		-0.71%	-0.71%
4		-0.43%	-0.43%
5	0.26%		0.26%
6	0.39%		0.39%
7	0.42%		0.42%
8		-0.06%	-0.06%
9		-0.34%	-0.34%
10	0.65%		0.65%
11	0.51%		0.51%
12	0.59%		0.59%
13	0.10%		0.10%
14	0.83%		0.83%
15		-0.02%	-0.02%
16	0.43%		0.43%
17	0.96%		0.96%
18	0.60%		0.60%
19		-0.60%	-0.60%
20		-0.09%	-0.09%
21		-0.55%	-0.55%
22	0.05%		0.05%
23	0.07%		0.07%
24		-0.02%	-0.02%
25		-0.29%	-0.29%
26		-0.46%	-0.46%
27	0.38%		0.38%

Week No.	BUY	SELL	Buy & Hold
27	0.38%		0.38%
28	0.09%		0.09%
29	0.51%		0.51%
30	0.24%		0.24%
31		-0.46%	-0.46%
32	0.05%		0.05%
33	0.16%		0.16%
34		-0.25%	-0.25%
35		-0.09%	-0.09%
36	0.01%		0.01%
37	0.08%		0.08%
38		-0.11%	-0.11%
39		-0.69%	-0.69%
40	0.19%		0.19%
41	0.25%		0.25%
42	-0.40%		-0.40%
43	-0.12%		-0.12%
44	1.71%		1.71%
45	0.34%		0.34%
46	0.22%		0.22%
47	0.39%		0.39%
48	0.50%		0.50%
49	1.14%		1.14%
50	-0.60%		-0.60%
51	0.32%		0.32%
52	0.66%		0.66%
53	-0.09%		-0.09%
Averages	0.36%	-0.15%	0.13%

HISTORICAL YEARLY RETURNS

Year	Market Value Buy & Hold Strategy	Market Value Trading Strategy	Annual Returns Buy & Hold Strategy	Annual Returns Trading Strategy	Win
1997	$ 10,000	$ 10,000	0%	0%	Y
1998	$ 11,776	$ 12,285	18%	23%	Y
1999	$ 15,040	$ 17,461	28%	42%	Y
2000	$ 14,130	$ 19,357	-6%	11%	Y
2001	$ 13,428	$ 22,588	-5%	17%	Y
2002	$ 11,454	$ 21,432	-15%	-5%	Y
2003	$ 14,650	$ 28,592	28%	33%	Y
2004	$ 15,386	$ 28,575	5%	0%	N
2005	$ 15,634	$ 28,394	2%	-1%	N
2006	$ 18,591	$ 33,004	19%	16%	N
2007	$ 20,226	$ 34,732	9%	5%	N
2008	$ 13,726	$ 28,001	-32%	-19%	Y
2009	$ 16,848	$ 37,669	23%	35%	Y
2010	$ 19,208	$ 45,236	14%	20%	Y
2011	$ 20,756	$ 58,682	8%	30%	Y
2012	$ 22,818	$ 60,145	10%	2%	N
2013	$ 29,582	$ 75,512	30%	26%	N
2014	$ 32,487	$ 80,100	10%	6%	N
2015	$ 32,516	$ 83,723	0%	5%	Y
2016	$ 37,840	$ 97,988	16%	17%	Y
2017	$ 48,503	$ 112,458	28%	15%	N
Averages	-	-	9.0%	13.2%	61.9%

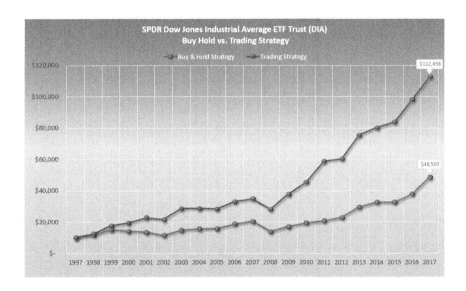

ISHARES REAL ESTATE 50 ETF (FTY)

SUMMARY

Ticker: FTY

Description: The investment seeks to track the investment results of the FTSE NAREIT Real Estate 50 Index composed of 50 of the largest U.S. real estate equities. The fund generally will invest at least 90% of its assets in the component securities of the underlying index and may invest up to 10% of its assets in certain futures, options and swap contracts, cash and cash equivalents. The underlying index is comprised of the 50 largest real estate investment trusts ("REITs") within the FTSE NAREIT Composite Index.

Data From: 1/2/2008 To: 12/28/2017		Total Return		
Winning Probability		• Buy & Hold:		83.54%
• Monthly:	66.67%	• Trading Strategy:		864.18%
• Annually:	63.64%	Trading Weeks:		
		BUY	**SELL**	
Average Annual Returns		11	18	
• Buy & Hold:	7.41%			
• Trading Strategy:	28.54%	28	39	
• Delta:	21.13%	48	1	

MONTHLY ANALYSIS

Month	Average Return Buy & Hold Strategy	Average Return Trading Strategy	Standard Dev of Month Return (Volatility)	Percentage Wins
Jan	-0.49%	0.00%	6.04%	50.00%
Feb	-1.29%	0.00%	7.90%	50.00%
Mar	4.09%	5.46%	4.55%	60.00%
Apr	4.53%	4.90%	8.97%	70.00%
May	-1.31%	0.00%	3.88%	60.00%
Jun	-1.04%	0.00%	5.54%	50.00%
Jul	3.12%	4.28%	3.74%	70.00%
Aug	-1.07%	-1.07%	5.45%	100.00%
Sep	0.19%	2.50%	5.49%	80.00%
Oct	0.31%	0.00%	13.03%	40.00%
Nov	-1.98%	3.44%	6.49%	70.00%
Dec	6.68%	6.68%	11.75%	100.00%
Averages	0.98%	2.18%	7.63%	66.67%

Figures from: 12/31/2007 to: 12/28/2017

WEEKLY AVERAGE RETURNS

Week No.	BUY	sell	Buy & Hold
1		-0.70%	-0.70%
2		-0.43%	-0.43%
3		0.25%	0.25%
4		0.86%	0.86%
5		0.52%	0.52%
6		-0.77%	-0.77%
7		-1.11%	-1.11%
8		0.87%	0.87%
9		-0.25%	-0.25%
10		-1.37%	-1.37%
11	3.36%		3.36%
12	1.33%		1.33%
13	-1.08%		-1.08%
14	2.88%		2.88%
15	-0.38%		-0.38%
16	1.22%		1.22%
17	3.04%		3.04%
18		-0.32%	-0.32%
19		-0.96%	-0.96%
20		-1.05%	-1.05%
21		-2.33%	-2.33%
22		0.51%	0.51%
23		-0.34%	-0.34%
24		0.92%	0.92%
25		-0.43%	-0.43%
26		-0.03%	-0.03%
27		-0.42%	-0.42%

Week No.	BUY	sell	Buy & Hold
27		-0.42%	-0.42%
28	1.10%		1.10%
29	0.81%		0.81%
30	1.37%		1.37%
31	0.12%		0.12%
32	0.04%		0.04%
33	-0.07%		-0.07%
34	0.08%		0.08%
35	1.28%		1.28%
36	0.23%		0.23%
37	-0.55%		-0.55%
38	1.71%		1.71%
39		-0.82%	-0.82%
40		-1.33%	-1.33%
41		-0.38%	-0.38%
42		-0.58%	-0.58%
43		-1.19%	-1.19%
44		0.87%	0.87%
45		-1.31%	-1.31%
46		-1.69%	-1.69%
47		-2.24%	-2.24%
48	0.40%		0.40%
49	3.60%		3.60%
50	-0.61%		-0.61%
51	1.47%		1.47%
52	1.08%		1.08%
53	0.76%		0.76%
Averages	0.97%	-0.52%	0.15%

| | Market Value | | Annual Returns | | |
Year	Buy & Hold Strategy	Trading Strategy	Buy & Hold Strategy	Trading Strategy	Win
2007	$ 10,000	$ 10,000	0%	0%	Y
2008	$ 6,284	$ 20,096	-37%	101%	Y
2009	$ 7,975	$ 46,964	27%	134%	Y
2010	$ 10,063	$ 65,148	26%	39%	Y
2011	$ 10,987	$ 67,268	9%	3%	N
2012	$ 12,823	$ 75,251	17%	12%	N
2013	$ 12,697	$ 79,770	-1%	6%	Y
2014	$ 16,395	$ 84,738	29%	6%	N
2015	$ 17,030	$ 89,799	4%	6%	Y
2016	$ 18,029	$ 93,891	6%	5%	N
2017	$ 18,354	$ 96,418	2%	3%	Y
Averages	-	-	7.4%	28.5%	63.6%

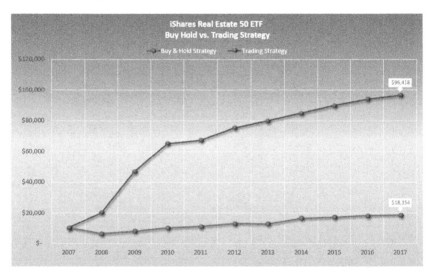

iShares Real Estate 50 ETF
Buy Hold vs. Trading Strategy

38

ISHARES U.S. HEALTHCARE ETF (IYH)

SUMMARY

Ticker: IYH

Description: The investment seeks to track the investment results of an index composed of U.S. equities in the healthcare sector. The fund generally invests at least 90% of its assets in securities of the underlying index and in depositary receipts representing securities of the underlying index. The underlying index measures the performance of the healthcare sector of the U.S. equity market. The fund is non-diversified.

Data From: 1/2/2001 To: 12/28/2017		Total Return		
Winning Probability		• Buy & Hold:		199.30%
• Monthly:	90.69%	• Trading Strategy:		258.47%
• Annually:	50.00%	Trading Weeks:		
		BUY	**SELL**	
Average Annual Returns		42	36	
• Buy & Hold:	7.49%			
• Trading Strategy:	8.15%			
• Delta:	0.66%			

⚠ NOTE: Due to the very low delta and the low annual winning probability, it is marginal to use the trading strategy versus the buy and hold method. Some industries do not have any seasonal trending.

MONTHLY ANALYSIS

Month	Average Return Buy & Hold Strategy	Average Return Trading Strategy	Standard Dev of Month Return (Volatility)	Percentage Wins
Jan	-0.58%	-0.58%	3.43%	100.00%
Feb	-0.03%	-0.03%	4.38%	100.00%
Mar	0.64%	0.64%	4.43%	100.00%
Apr	1.08%	1.08%	3.76%	100.00%
May	0.41%	0.41%	3.32%	100.00%
Jun	-0.02%	-0.02%	3.49%	100.00%
Jul	1.19%	1.19%	3.67%	100.00%
Aug	-0.04%	-0.09%	3.51%	88.24%
Sep	-0.04%	0.00%	3.22%	47.06%
Oct	0.05%	1.01%	5.02%	52.94%
Nov	1.60%	1.60%	3.54%	100.00%
Dec	1.48%	1.48%	4.01%	100.00%
Averages	0.48%	0.56%	3.81%	90.69%

Figures from: 12/29/2000 to: 12/28/2017

WEEKLY AVERAGE RETURNS

Week No.	BUY	SELL	Buy & Hold	Week No.	BUY	SELL	Buy & Hold
1	-0.38%		-0.38%	27	0.31%		0.31%
2	0.38%		0.38%	28	0.15%		0.15%
3	-0.37%		-0.37%	29	0.29%		0.29%
4	-0.16%		-0.16%	30	1.02%		1.02%
5	0.43%		0.43%	31	-0.10%		-0.10%
6	0.12%		0.12%	32	-0.18%		-0.18%
7	0.38%		0.38%	33	0.17%		0.17%
8	0.11%		0.11%	34	-0.06%		-0.06%
9	-0.40%		-0.40%	35	0.12%		0.12%
10	0.34%		0.34%	36		0.04%	0.04%
11	0.02%		0.02%	37		0.33%	0.33%
12	-0.20%		-0.20%	38		-0.17%	-0.17%
13	0.39%		0.39%	39		-0.09%	-0.09%
14	0.35%		0.35%	40		0.63%	0.63%
15	0.10%		0.10%	41		-0.59%	-0.59%
16	0.84%		0.84%	42	0.11%		0.11%
17	0.49%		0.49%	43	-0.74%		-0.74%
18	0.17%		0.17%	44	0.89%		0.89%
19	-0.60%		-0.60%	45	-0.24%		-0.24%
20	0.08%		0.08%	46	0.75%		0.75%
21	-0.38%		-0.38%	47	-0.19%		-0.19%
22	0.65%		0.65%	48	0.57%		0.57%
23	0.08%		0.08%	49	1.15%		1.15%
24	0.17%		0.17%	50	-0.60%		-0.60%
25	0.13%		0.13%	51	1.12%		1.12%
26	0.09%		0.09%	52	0.34%		0.34%
27	0.31%		0.31%	53	0.00%		0.00%
				Averages	0.17%	0.02%	0.15%

HISTORICAL YEARLY RETURNS

Year	Market Value Buy & Hold Strategy	Market Value Trading Strategy	Annual Returns Buy & Hold Strategy	Annual Returns Trading Strategy	Win
2000	$ 10,000	$ 10,000	0%	0%	Y
2001	$ 8,670	$ 8,777	-13%	-12%	Y
2002	$ 6,824	$ 7,143	-21%	-19%	Y
2003	$ 8,091	$ 8,335	19%	17%	N
2004	$ 8,432	$ 9,040	4%	8%	Y
2005	$ 9,079	$ 9,825	8%	9%	Y
2006	$ 9,638	$ 10,324	6%	5%	N
2007	$ 10,410	$ 10,550	8%	2%	N
2008	$ 8,027	$ 10,737	-23%	2%	Y
2009	$ 9,710	$ 12,768	21%	19%	N
2010	$ 10,110	$ 12,235	4%	-4%	N
2011	$ 11,248	$ 13,670	11%	12%	Y
2012	$ 13,354	$ 15,563	19%	14%	N
2013	$ 18,863	$ 21,131	41%	36%	N
2014	$ 23,606	$ 26,903	25%	27%	Y
2015	$ 25,062	$ 30,276	6%	13%	Y
2016	$ 24,387	$ 29,724	-3%	-2%	Y
2017	$ 29,930	$ 35,847	23%	21%	N
Averages	-	-	7.5%	8.2%	50.0%

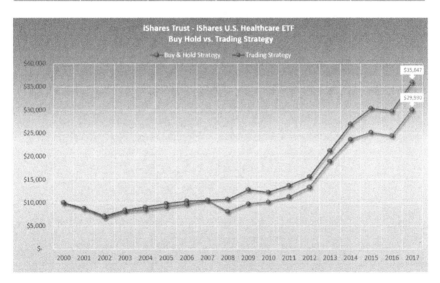

iShares Trust - iShares U.S. Healthcare ETF
Buy Hold vs. Trading Strategy

41

ISHARES NORTH AMERICAN TECH ETF (IGM)

SUMMARY

Ticker: IGM

Description: The investment seeks to track the investment results of an index composed of North American equities in the technology sector. The fund generally invests at least 90% of its assets in securities of the underlying index and in depositary receipts representing securities of the underlying index. The underlying index measures the performance of U.S.-traded stocks of technology-related companies in the United States and Canada. Components primarily include information technology and technology companies. The fund is non-diversified.

Data From: 3/19/2001 To: 12/28/2017		Total Return		
Winning Probability		• Buy & Hold:		245.58%
• Monthly:	84.65%	• Trading Strategy:		417.46%
• Annually:	72.22%	Trading Weeks:		
		BUY		**SELL**
Average Annual Returns		6		1
• Buy & Hold:	10.52%			
• Trading Strategy:	12.35%	25		23
• Delta:	1.8%	33		31

MONTHLY ANALYSIS

Month	Average Return Buy & Hold Strategy	Average Return Trading Strategy	Standard Dev of Month Return (Volatility)	Percentage Wins
Jan	-1.80%	-0.61%	5.24%	50.00%
Feb	-0.09%	-0.09%	5.00%	100.00%
Mar	1.34%	1.34%	4.70%	100.00%
Apr	1.82%	1.82%	8.06%	100.00%
May	0.98%	0.91%	6.02%	88.24%
Jun	-1.71%	-0.53%	4.18%	58.82%
Jul	0.88%	0.65%	5.49%	52.94%
Aug	-0.22%	0.53%	6.29%	64.71%
Sep	-1.00%	-1.00%	7.57%	100.00%
Oct	4.57%	4.57%	8.59%	100.00%
Nov	2.42%	2.42%	5.82%	100.00%
Dec	0.45%	0.45%	5.17%	100.00%
Averages	0.64%	0.87%	6.24%	84.65%

Figures from: 03/19/2001 to: 12/28/2017

WEEKLY AVERAGE RETURNS

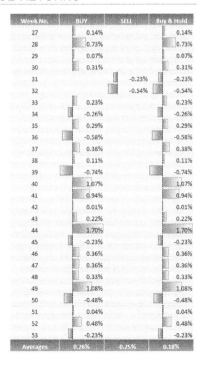

Week No.	BUY	SELL	Buy & Hold
1		0.78%	0.78%
2		-0.12%	-0.12%
3		-1.17%	-1.17%
4		0.13%	0.13%
5	-0.39%		-0.39%
6	0.41%		0.41%
7	0.71%		0.71%
8	-0.25%		-0.25%
9	0.14%		0.14%
10	0.56%		0.56%
11	0.67%		0.67%
12	0.67%		0.67%
13	-0.39%		-0.39%
14	0.71%		0.71%
15	0.34%		0.34%
16	1.68%		1.68%
17	0.86%		0.86%
18	0.08%		0.08%
19	-0.93%		-0.93%
20	0.56%		0.56%
21	-0.54%		-0.54%
22	0.56%		0.56%
23		-0.06%	-0.06%
24		-0.52%	-0.52%
25	-0.68%		-0.68%
26	0.32%		0.32%
27	0.14%		0.14%

Week No.	BUY	SELL	Buy & Hold
27	0.14%		0.14%
28	0.73%		0.73%
29	0.07%		0.07%
30	0.31%		0.31%
31		-0.23%	-0.23%
32		-0.54%	-0.54%
33	0.23%		0.23%
34	-0.26%		-0.26%
35	0.29%		0.29%
36	-0.58%		-0.58%
37	0.38%		0.38%
38	0.11%		0.11%
39	-0.74%		-0.74%
40	1.07%		1.07%
41	0.94%		0.94%
42	0.01%		0.01%
43	0.22%		0.22%
44	1.70%		1.70%
45	-0.23%		-0.23%
46	0.36%		0.36%
47	0.36%		0.36%
48	0.33%		0.33%
49	1.08%		1.08%
50	-0.48%		-0.48%
51	0.04%		0.04%
52	0.48%		0.48%
53	-0.23%		-0.23%
Averages	0.26%	-0.25%	0.18%

HISTORICAL YEARLY RETURNS

Year	Market Value		Annual Returns		Win
	Buy & Hold Strategy	Trading Strategy	Buy & Hold Strategy	Trading Strategy	
2000	$ 10,000	$ 10,000	0%	0%	Y
2001	$ 9,501	$ 10,509	-5%	5%	Y
2002	$ 5,631	$ 6,627	-41%	-37%	Y
2003	$ 8,594	$ 10,426	53%	57%	Y
2004	$ 8,828	$ 10,303	3%	-1%	N
2005	$ 8,963	$ 11,443	2%	11%	Y
2006	$ 9,743	$ 12,505	9%	9%	Y
2007	$ 11,313	$ 14,551	16%	16%	Y
2008	$ 6,396	$ 9,325	-43%	-36%	Y
2009	$ 10,389	$ 14,532	62%	56%	N
2010	$ 11,633	$ 17,129	12%	18%	Y
2011	$ 11,502	$ 19,323	-1%	13%	Y
2012	$ 13,182	$ 19,094	15%	-1%	N
2013	$ 17,659	$ 24,330	34%	27%	N
2014	$ 20,276	$ 28,445	15%	17%	Y
2015	$ 22,201	$ 31,566	9%	11%	Y
2016	$ 25,073	$ 37,953	13%	20%	Y
2017	$ 34,558	$ 51,746	38%	36%	N
Averages	-	-	10.5%	12.3%	72.2%

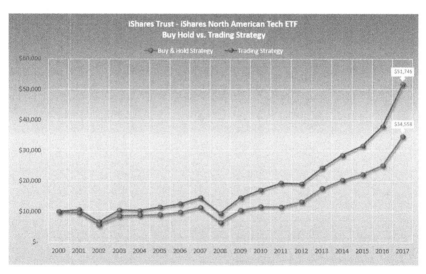

ISHARES U.S. ENERGY ETF (IYE)

SUMMARY

Ticker: IYE

Description: The investment seeks to track the investment results of the Dow Jones U.S. Oil & Gas Index composed of U.S. equities in the energy sector. The fund generally invests at least 90% of its assets in securities of the underlying index and in depositary receipts representing securities of the underlying index. The underlying index measures the performance of the oil and gas sector of the U.S. equity market. The fund is non-diversified.

Data From: 6/16/2000 To: 12/28/2017		Total Return		
Winning Probability		• Buy & Hold:		205.08%
• Monthly:	73.46%	• Trading Strategy:		682.60%
• Annually:	63.16%	Trading Weeks:		
		BUY	**SELL**	
Average Annual Returns		4	1	
• Buy & Hold:	8.17%			
• Trading Strategy:	12.39%	32	21	
• Delta:	4.22%	42	39	

MONTHLY ANALYSIS

Month	Average Return Buy & Hold Strategy	Average Return Trading Strategy	Standard Dev of Month Return (Volatility)	Percentage Wins
Jan	-1.50%	0.67%	5.93%	52.94%
Feb	1.74%	1.74%	5.85%	100.00%
Mar	1.77%	1.77%	4.45%	100.00%
Apr	2.62%	2.62%	5.70%	100.00%
May	-0.52%	-0.80%	6.55%	52.94%
Jun	-0.20%	0.00%	4.78%	44.44%
Jul	-0.91%	-0.03%	5.95%	44.44%
Aug	0.24%	0.67%	5.72%	94.44%
Sep	-0.08%	0.85%	6.52%	55.56%
Oct	0.81%	1.67%	8.39%	38.89%
Nov	0.91%	0.91%	4.97%	100.00%
Dec	2.16%	2.16%	5.49%	100.00%
Averages	0.59%	1.02%	5.92%	73.46%

Figures from: 06/16/2000 to: 12/28/2017

WEEKLY AVERAGE RETURNS

Week No.	BUY	SELL	Buy & Hold
1		-0.58%	-0.58%
2		-1.16%	-1.16%
3		-0.10%	-0.10%
4	0.70%		0.70%
5	0.74%		0.74%
6	0.25%		0.25%
7	0.59%		0.59%
8	0.21%		0.21%
9	0.36%		0.36%
10	0.85%		0.85%
11	-0.34%		-0.34%
12	0.39%		0.39%
13	-0.01%		-0.01%
14	1.10%		1.10%
15	-0.27%		-0.27%
16	0.85%		0.85%
17	1.36%		1.36%
18	0.07%		0.07%
19	-0.99%		-0.99%
20	-0.21%		-0.21%
21		-0.58%	-0.58%
22		0.60%	0.60%
23		-0.22%	-0.22%
24		1.01%	1.01%
25		-0.20%	-0.20%
26		-0.03%	-0.03%
27		-0.07%	-0.07%

Week No.	BUY	SELL	Buy & Hold
27		-0.07%	-0.07%
28		-0.16%	-0.16%
29		0.16%	0.16%
30		0.60%	0.60%
31		-1.02%	-1.02%
32	0.33%		0.33%
33	0.47%		0.47%
34	0.03%		0.03%
35	0.70%		0.70%
36	0.21%		0.21%
37	0.63%		0.63%
38	0.34%		0.34%
39		-0.76%	-0.76%
40		0.76%	0.76%
41		-0.50%	-0.50%
42	-0.03%		-0.03%
43	-0.37%		-0.37%
44	1.00%		1.00%
45	0.93%		0.93%
46	-0.88%		-0.88%
47	0.72%		0.72%
48	0.46%		0.46%
49	0.47%		0.47%
50	-0.30%		-0.30%
51	1.07%		1.07%
52	1.09%		1.09%
53	0.17%		0.17%
Averages	0.35%	-0.13%	0.20%

	Market Value		Annual Returns		
Year	Buy & Hold Strategy	Trading Strategy	Buy & Hold Strategy	Trading Strategy	Win
1999	$ 10,000	$ 10,000	0%	0%	Y
2000	$ 10,675	$ 12,429	7%	24%	Y
2001	$ 9,373	$ 12,930	-12%	4%	Y
2002	$ 7,867	$ 14,712	-16%	14%	Y
2003	$ 10,079	$ 18,401	28%	25%	N
2004	$ 13,279	$ 20,966	32%	14%	N
2005	$ 17,882	$ 24,563	35%	17%	N
2006	$ 21,485	$ 23,423	20%	-5%	N
2007	$ 29,164	$ 33,104	36%	41%	Y
2008	$ 18,306	$ 47,285	-37%	43%	Y
2009	$ 21,831	$ 53,527	19%	13%	N
2010	$ 25,976	$ 59,613	19%	11%	N
2011	$ 26,935	$ 63,110	4%	6%	Y
2012	$ 28,082	$ 59,612	4%	-6%	N
2013	$ 35,302	$ 69,290	26%	16%	N
2014	$ 31,894	$ 70,269	-10%	1%	Y
2015	$ 24,821	$ 60,668	-22%	-14%	Y
2016	$ 31,162	$ 77,391	26%	28%	Y
2017	$ 30,508	$ 78,260	-2%	1%	Y
Averages	-	-	8.2%	12.4%	63.2%

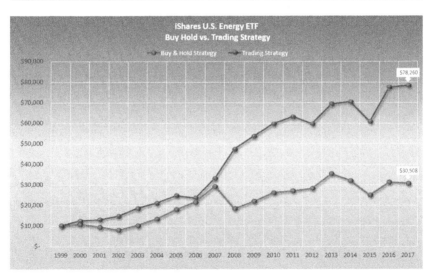

ISHARES GOLD TRUST (IAU)

SUMMARY

Ticker: IAU

Description: The investment seeks to reflect generally the performance of the price of gold. The Trust seeks to reflect such performance before payment of the Trust's expenses and liabilities. The Trust is not actively managed. It does not engage in any activities designed to obtain a profit from, or to ameliorate losses caused by, changes in the price of gold. The Trust receives gold deposited with it in exchange for the creation of Baskets of Shares, sells gold as necessary to cover the Trust expenses and other liabilities and delivers gold in exchange for Baskets of Shares surrendered to it for redemption.

Data From: 1/28/2005 To: 12/28/2017		Total Return		
Winning Probability		• Buy & Hold:		191.40%
• Monthly:	75.64%	• Trading Strategy:		326.65%
• Annually:	78.57%	Trading Weeks:		
		BUY	**SELL**	
Average Annual Returns		28	12	
• Buy & Hold:	9.17%			
• Trading Strategy:	11.51%	52	48	
• Delta:	2.33%			

MONTHLY ANALYSIS

Month	Average Return Buy & Hold Strategy	Average Return Trading Strategy	Standard Dev of Month Return (Volatility)	Percentage Wins
Jan	3.04%	3.04%	4.68%	100.00%
Feb	2.14%	2.14%	4.75%	100.00%
Mar	-1.07%	-0.43%	2.69%	38.46%
Apr	1.68%	0.00%	5.20%	38.46%
May	-0.53%	0.00%	4.61%	61.54%
Jun	-0.36%	0.00%	5.62%	61.54%
Jul	0.84%	1.24%	4.02%	84.62%
Aug	1.88%	1.88%	5.47%	100.00%
Sep	0.49%	0.49%	6.26%	100.00%
Oct	-0.15%	-0.15%	5.91%	100.00%
Nov	1.53%	1.78%	6.40%	46.15%
Dec	-0.23%	1.24%	6.15%	76.92%
Averages	0.77%	0.94%	5.20%	75.64%

Figures from: 01/28/2005 to: 12/28/2017

WEEKLY AVERAGE RETURNS

Week No.	BUY	SELL	Buy & Hold	Week No.	BUY	SELL	Buy & Hold
1	-0.05%		-0.05%	27		-0.72%	-0.72%
2	1.27%		1.27%	28	1.53%		1.53%
3	0.24%		0.24%	29	-0.13%		-0.13%
4	0.50%		0.50%	30	0.04%		0.04%
5	0.10%		0.10%	31	0.01%		0.01%
6	-0.01%		-0.01%	32	0.28%		0.28%
7	1.20%		1.20%	33	0.12%		0.12%
8	1.08%		1.08%	34	1.32%		1.32%
9	-0.74%		-0.74%	35	0.24%		0.24%
10	-0.13%		-0.13%	36	0.80%		0.80%
11	0.49%		0.49%	37		-0.92%	-0.92%
12		-0.20%	-0.20%	38	1.54%		1.54%
13		-0.16%	-0.16%	39	-0.30%		-0.30%
14		0.01%	0.01%	40	-0.92%		-0.92%
15	0.81%		0.81%	41	0.40%		0.40%
16		-0.12%	-0.12%	42	-0.32%		-0.32%
17	0.86%		0.86%	43	-0.64%		-0.64%
18	0.35%		0.35%	44	0.23%		0.23%
19		-0.25%	-0.25%	45	0.91%		0.91%
20	0.22%		0.22%	46	-0.23%		-0.23%
21		-0.25%	-0.25%	47	1.35%		1.35%
22	0.44%		0.44%	48		-1.01%	-1.01%
23		-0.87%	-0.87%	49		-0.19%	-0.19%
24		-0.23%	-0.23%	50		-0.07%	-0.07%
25	0.66%		0.66%	51		-1.12%	-1.12%
26	0.77%		0.77%	52	1.03%		1.03%
27		-0.72%	-0.72%	53	0.25%		0.25%
				Averages	0.32%	-0.05%	0.18%

49

HISTORICAL YEARLY RETURNS

Year	Market Value Buy & Hold Strategy	Market Value Trading Strategy	Annual Returns Buy & Hold Strategy	Annual Returns Trading Strategy	Win
2004	$ 10,000	$ 10,000	0%	0%	Y
2005	$ 12,118	$ 12,192	21%	22%	Y
2006	$ 14,816	$ 13,528	22%	11%	N
2007	$ 19,314	$ 17,821	30%	32%	Y
2008	$ 20,300	$ 19,315	5%	8%	Y
2009	$ 25,151	$ 24,754	24%	28%	Y
2010	$ 32,560	$ 28,764	29%	16%	N
2011	$ 35,676	$ 32,476	10%	13%	Y
2012	$ 38,135	$ 38,577	7%	19%	Y
2013	$ 27,360	$ 37,365	-28%	-3%	Y
2014	$ 26,798	$ 38,538	-2%	3%	Y
2015	$ 23,963	$ 34,522	-11%	-10%	Y
2016	$ 25,955	$ 37,061	8%	7%	N
2017	$ 29,140	$ 42,665	12%	15%	Y
Averages	-	-	**9.2%**	**11.5%**	**78.6%**

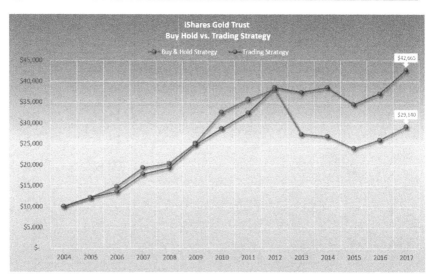

ISHARES U.S. FINANCIALS ETF (IYF)

SUMMARY

Ticker: IYF

Description: The investment seeks to track the investment results of an index composed of U.S. equities in the financial sector. The fund generally invests at least 90% of its assets in securities of the underlying index and in depositary receipts representing securities of the underlying index. It seeks to track the investment results of the Dow Jones U.S. Financials Index (the "underlying index"), which measures the performance of the financial sector of the U.S. equity market. The fund is non-diversified.

Data From: 5/26/2000 To: 12/28/2017		Total Return		
Winning Probability		• Buy & Hold:		83.27%
• Monthly:	77.36%	• Trading Strategy:		347.22%
• Annually:	73.68%	Trading Weeks:		
		BUY	**SELL**	
Average Annual Returns		10	1	
• Buy & Hold:	5.50%	26	19	
• Trading Strategy:	9.83%	36	32	
• Delta:	4.3%			

51

MONTHLY ANALYSIS

Month	Average Return Buy & Hold Strategy	Average Return Trading Strategy	Standard Dev of Month Return (Volatility)	Percentage Wins
Jan	-2.02%	0.00%	6.60%	58.82%
Feb	-1.14%	-0.08%	5.75%	41.18%
Mar	1.94%	2.11%	5.62%	94.12%
Apr	1.91%	1.91%	5.34%	100.00%
May	-0.95%	0.37%	7.12%	44.44%
Jun	-1.38%	0.00%	4.90%	61.11%
Jul	1.13%	1.50%	4.96%	61.11%
Aug	-0.04%	0.25%	5.62%	44.44%
Sep	-0.10%	-0.10%	4.29%	100.00%
Oct	1.11%	1.11%	7.77%	100.00%
Nov	0.85%	0.85%	5.49%	100.00%
Dec	3.12%	3.12%	5.83%	100.00%
Averages	0.37%	0.92%	5.89%	75.47%

Figures from: 05/26/2000 to: 12/28/2017

WEEKLY AVERAGE RETURNS

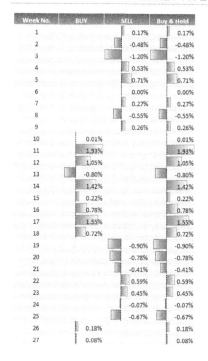

Week No.	BUY	SELL	Buy & Hold
1		0.17%	0.17%
2		-0.48%	-0.48%
3		-1.20%	-1.20%
4		0.53%	0.53%
5		0.71%	0.71%
6		0.00%	0.00%
7		0.27%	0.27%
8		-0.55%	-0.55%
9		0.26%	0.26%
10	0.01%		0.01%
11	1.93%		1.93%
12	1.05%		1.05%
13	-0.80%		-0.80%
14	1.42%		1.42%
15	0.22%		0.22%
16	0.78%		0.78%
17	1.55%		1.55%
18	0.72%		0.72%
19		-0.90%	-0.90%
20		-0.78%	-0.78%
21		-0.41%	-0.41%
22		0.59%	0.59%
23		0.45%	0.45%
24		-0.07%	-0.07%
25		-0.67%	-0.67%
26	0.18%		0.18%
27	0.08%		0.08%

Week No.	BUY	SELL	Buy & Hold
27	0.08%		0.08%
28	0.22%		0.22%
29	0.52%		0.52%
30	0.80%		0.80%
31	0.00%		0.00%
32		0.38%	0.38%
33		0.09%	0.09%
34		-0.54%	-0.54%
35		0.63%	0.63%
36	-0.19%		-0.19%
37	0.24%		0.24%
38	0.74%		0.74%
39	-0.43%		-0.43%
40	0.14%		0.14%
41	-0.10%		-0.10%
42	-0.50%		-0.50%
43	-0.07%		-0.07%
44	1.40%		1.40%
45	-0.26%		-0.26%
46	-0.09%		-0.09%
47	-0.95%		-0.95%
48	1.06%		1.06%
49	2.38%		2.38%
50	-0.70%		-0.70%
51	0.61%		0.61%
52	0.77%		0.77%
53	0.23%		0.23%
Averages	0.39%	-0.07%	0.22%

Year	Market Value		Annual Returns		Win
	Buy & Hold Strategy	Trading Strategy	Buy & Hold Strategy	Trading Strategy	
1999	$ 10,000	$ 10,000	0%	0%	Y
2000	$ 9,773	$ 11,615	-2%	16%	Y
2001	$ 9,135	$ 11,938	-7%	3%	Y
2002	$ 7,869	$ 10,400	-14%	-13%	Y
2003	$ 10,394	$ 13,396	32%	29%	N
2004	$ 11,746	$ 13,367	13%	0%	N
2005	$ 12,419	$ 14,188	6%	6%	Y
2006	$ 14,746	$ 17,351	19%	22%	Y
2007	$ 12,083	$ 14,391	-18%	-17%	Y
2008	$ 6,007	$ 9,821	-50%	-32%	Y
2009	$ 7,019	$ 14,277	17%	45%	Y
2010	$ 7,877	$ 18,273	12%	28%	Y
2011	$ 6,834	$ 18,833	-13%	3%	Y
2012	$ 8,606	$ 21,445	26%	14%	N
2013	$ 11,530	$ 28,239	34%	32%	N
2014	$ 13,165	$ 29,663	14%	5%	N
2015	$ 13,113	$ 30,667	0%	3%	Y
2016	$ 15,335	$ 39,717	17%	30%	Y
2017	$ 18,327	$ 44,722	20%	13%	N
Averages	-	-	5.5%	9.8%	73.7%

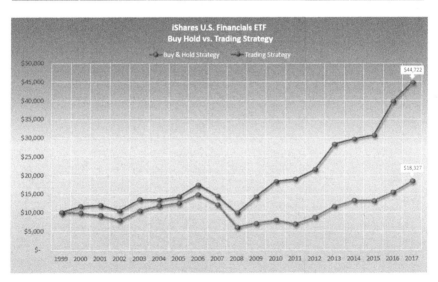

iShares U.S. Financials ETF
Buy Hold vs. Trading Strategy

Buy & Hold Strategy   Trading Strategy

53

ISHARES U.S. INDUSTRIALS ETF (IYJ)

SUMMARY

Ticker: IYJ

Description: The investment seeks to track the investment results of the Dow Jones U.S. Industrials Index composed of U.S. equities in the industrials sector. The fund generally invests at least 90% of its assets in securities of the underlying index and in depositary receipts representing securities of the underlying index. The underlying index measures the performance of the industrials sector of the U.S. equity market.

Data From: 7/14/2000 To: 12/28/2017		Total Return		
Winning Probability		• Buy & Hold:		206.97%
• Monthly:	90.48%	• Trading Strategy:		293.15%
• Annually:	73.68%	Trading Weeks:		
			BUY	SELL
Average Annual Returns			5	1
• Buy & Hold:	8.03%		23	19
• Trading Strategy:	9.33%			
• Delta:	1.30%			

MONTHLY ANALYSIS

Month	Average Return Buy & Hold Strategy	Average Return Trading Strategy	Standard Dev of Month Return (Volatility)	Percentage Wins
Jan	-1.42%	0.00%	5.30%	52.94%
Feb	0.13%	-0.05%	4.86%	35.29%
Mar	1.62%	1.80%	5.32%	94.12%
Apr	2.47%	2.47%	5.96%	100.00%
May	0.35%	0.38%	4.24%	29.41%
Jun	-1.25%	0.00%	3.94%	58.82%
Jul	0.05%	0.00%	5.13%	50.00%
Aug	0.01%	0.00%	4.53%	44.44%
Sep	-0.95%	-0.04%	6.38%	50.00%
Oct	1.34%	1.34%	7.12%	100.00%
Nov	2.37%	2.37%	4.72%	100.00%
Dec	2.28%	2.28%	3.86%	100.00%
Averages	0.58%	0.88%	5.24%	68.10%

Figures from: 07/14/2000 to: 12/28/2017

WEEKLY AVERAGE RETURNS

Week No.	BUY	SELL	Buy & Hold
1		0.23%	0.23%
2		-0.41%	-0.41%
3		-0.57%	-0.57%
4		-0.15%	-0.15%
5	0.29%		0.29%
6	0.33%		0.33%
7	0.61%		0.61%
8	-0.15%		-0.15%
9	-0.26%		-0.26%
10	0.42%		0.42%
11	0.74%		0.74%
12	0.48%		0.48%
13	0.05%		0.05%
14	0.94%		0.94%
15	-0.24%		-0.24%
16	1.45%		1.45%
17	1.33%		1.33%
18	0.60%		0.60%
19		-0.81%	-0.81%
20		-0.06%	-0.06%
21		-0.65%	-0.65%
22		0.59%	0.59%
23	-0.24%		-0.24%
24	0.41%		0.41%
25	-0.35%		-0.35%
26	-0.29%		-0.29%
27	-0.08%		-0.08%

Week No.	BUY	SELL	Buy & Hold
27	-0.08%		-0.08%
28	0.16%		0.16%
29	0.20%		0.20%
30	0.75%		0.75%
31	-0.67%		-0.67%
32	-0.17%		-0.17%
33	0.08%		0.08%
34	-0.05%		-0.05%
35	0.39%		0.39%
36	-0.07%		-0.07%
37	0.21%		0.21%
38	0.04%		0.04%
39	-0.92%		-0.92%
40	0.34%		0.34%
41	0.45%		0.45%
42	-0.32%		-0.32%
43	-0.21%		-0.21%
44	1.19%		1.19%
45	0.60%		0.60%
46	0.01%		0.01%
47	0.32%		0.32%
48	0.76%		0.76%
49	1.25%		1.25%
50	-0.28%		-0.28%
51	0.29%		0.29%
52	0.55%		0.55%
53	0.23%		0.23%
Averages	0.25%	-0.24%	0.18%

Year	Market Value		Annual Returns		Win
	Buy & Hold Strategy	Trading Strategy	Buy & Hold Strategy	Trading Strategy	
1999	$ 10,000	$ 10,000	0%	0%	Y
2000	$ 9,342	$ 9,342	-7%	-7%	Y
2001	$ 8,404	$ 8,335	-10%	-11%	N
2002	$ 6,282	$ 6,416	-25%	-23%	Y
2003	$ 8,331	$ 8,616	33%	34%	Y
2004	$ 9,693	$ 9,543	16%	11%	N
2005	$ 10,087	$ 10,109	4%	6%	Y
2006	$ 11,419	$ 11,767	13%	16%	Y
2007	$ 12,905	$ 12,786	13%	9%	N
2008	$ 7,772	$ 8,398	-40%	-34%	Y
2009	$ 9,779	$ 11,568	26%	38%	Y
2010	$ 12,271	$ 16,069	25%	39%	Y
2011	$ 12,124	$ 15,983	-1%	-1%	Y
2012	$ 14,215	$ 18,707	17%	17%	N
2013	$ 19,911	$ 23,739	40%	27%	N
2014	$ 21,249	$ 26,051	7%	10%	Y
2015	$ 20,829	$ 25,838	-2%	-1%	Y
2016	$ 24,763	$ 33,306	19%	29%	Y
2017	$ 30,697	$ 39,315	24%	18%	N
Averages	-	-	8.0%	9.3%	73.7%

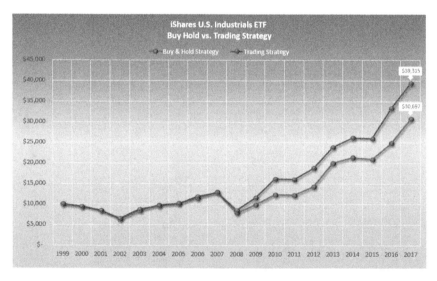

ISHARES TRANSPORTATION AVERAGE ETF (IYT)

SUMMARY

Ticker: IYT

Description: The investment seeks to track the investment results of the Dow Jones Transportation Average Index composed of U.S. equities in the transportation sector. The fund generally invests at least 90% of its assets in securities of the underlying index and in depositary receipts representing securities of the underlying index. The underlying index measures the performance of the transportation sector of the U.S. equity market.

Data From: 1/2/2004 To: 12/28/2017		Total Return		
Winning Probability		• Buy & Hold:		310.25%
• Monthly:	89.88%	• Trading Strategy:		695.25%
• Annually:	66.67%	Trading Weeks:		
		BUY	**SELL**	
Average Annual Returns		4	1	
• Buy & Hold:	11.96%			
• Trading Strategy:	17.24%	22	19	
• Delta:	5.28%	35	32	

MONTHLY ANALYSIS

Month	Average Return Buy & Hold Strategy	Average Return Trading Strategy	Standard Dev of Month Return (Volatility)	Percentage Wins
Jan	-1.34%	0.07%	7.11%	50.00%
Feb	0.43%	0.43%	5.21%	100.00%
Mar	2.64%	2.64%	5.20%	100.00%
Apr	1.81%	1.81%	5.07%	100.00%
May	0.51%	2.28%	4.06%	71.43%
Jun	-0.60%	-0.60%	4.77%	100.00%
Jul	0.83%	0.83%	6.51%	100.00%
Aug	-1.93%	0.29%	4.22%	57.14%
Sep	0.98%	0.98%	5.00%	100.00%
Oct	2.73%	2.73%	7.70%	100.00%
Nov	2.91%	2.91%	5.63%	100.00%
Dec	1.59%	1.59%	4.30%	100.00%
Averages	0.88%	1.33%	5.54%	89.88%

Figures from: 01/02/2004 to: 12/28/2017

WEEKLY AVERAGE RETURNS

Week No.	BUY	SELL	Buy & Hold
1		-0.14%	-0.14%
2		-0.42%	-0.42%
3		-0.57%	-0.57%
4	0.54%		0.54%
5	0.06%		0.06%
6	1.04%		1.04%
7	0.76%		0.76%
8	0.06%		0.06%
9	-0.18%		-0.18%
10	0.28%		0.28%
11	1.57%		1.57%
12	0.43%		0.43%
13	-0.01%		-0.01%
14	1.48%		1.48%
15	-0.57%		-0.57%
16	1.65%		1.65%
17	1.04%		1.04%
18	1.23%		1.23%
19		-1.42%	-1.42%
20		-1.25%	-1.25%
21		-0.39%	-0.39%
22	1.23%		1.23%
23	-0.19%		-0.19%
24	0.40%		0.40%
25	0.57%		0.57%
26	-0.03%		-0.03%
27	0.07%		0.07%

Week No.	BUY	SELL	Buy & Hold
27	0.07%		0.07%
28	0.91%		0.91%
29	0.74%		0.74%
30	0.27%		0.27%
31	0.13%		0.13%
32		-1.34%	-1.34%
33		-0.20%	-0.20%
34		-0.61%	-0.61%
35	0.68%		0.68%
36	0.16%		0.16%
37	1.19%		1.19%
38	0.58%		0.58%
39	-0.73%		-0.73%
40	0.29%		0.29%
41	0.35%		0.35%
42	0.22%		0.22%
43	0.01%		0.01%
44	0.78%		0.78%
45	0.26%		0.26%
46	-0.08%		-0.08%
47	-0.27%		-0.27%
48	1.23%		1.23%
49	2.14%		2.14%
50	-1.39%		-1.39%
51	0.48%		0.48%
52	0.98%		0.98%
53	0.17%		0.17%
Averages	0.47%	-0.72%	0.27%

HISTORICAL YEARLY RETURNS

| Year | Market Value | | Annual Returns | | Win |
	Buy & Hold Strategy	Trading Strategy	Buy & Hold Strategy	Trading Strategy	
2004	$ 12,677	$ 12,935	27%	29%	Y
2005	$ 14,056	$ 14,770	11%	14%	Y
2006	$ 15,318	$ 17,906	9%	21%	Y
2007	$ 15,378	$ 16,691	0%	-7%	N
2008	$ 12,113	$ 14,390	-21%	-14%	Y
2009	$ 14,411	$ 19,140	19%	33%	Y
2010	$ 18,261	$ 27,486	27%	44%	Y
2011	$ 17,980	$ 32,713	-2%	19%	Y
2012	$ 19,177	$ 33,780	7%	3%	N
2013	$ 27,073	$ 44,279	41%	31%	N
2014	$ 33,939	$ 51,026	25%	15%	N
2015	$ 28,199	$ 48,398	-17%	-5%	Y
2016	$ 34,447	$ 67,111	22%	39%	Y
2017	$ 41,025	$ 79,525	19%	18%	N
Averages	-	-	12.0%	17.2%	66.7%

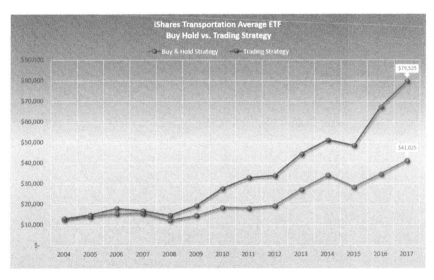

ISHARES U.S. BASIC MATERIALS ETF (IYM)

SUMMARY

Ticker: IYM

Description: The investment seeks to track the investment results of the Dow Jones U.S. Basic Materials Index composed of U.S. equities in the basic materials sector. The fund generally invests at least 90% of its assets in securities of the underlying index and in depositary receipts representing securities of the underlying index. The underlying index measures the performance of the basic materials sector of the U.S. equity market. The fund is non-diversified.

Data From: 6/20/2000 To: 12/28/2017		Total Return		
Winning Probability		• Buy & Hold:		301.43%
• Monthly:	85.31%	• Trading Strategy:		667.10%
• Annually:	84.21%	Trading Weeks:		
		BUY	**SELL**	
Average Annual Returns		4	1	
• Buy & Hold:	11.07%	21	19	
• Trading Strategy:	14.58%	33	31	
• Delta:	3.51%			

60

MONTHLY ANALYSIS

Month	Average Return Buy & Hold Strategy	Average Return Trading Strategy	Standard Dev of Month Return (Volatility)	Percentage Wins
Jan	-2.06%	0.36%	5.74%	70.59%
Feb	1.69%	1.69%	4.82%	100.00%
Mar	1.97%	1.97%	6.85%	100.00%
Apr	2.09%	2.09%	5.64%	100.00%
May	0.81%	1.76%	5.79%	58.82%
Jun	-1.18%	-1.18%	3.66%	100.00%
Jul	0.61%	0.41%	6.69%	38.89%
Aug	-0.42%	0.66%	3.30%	55.56%
Sep	-2.40%	-2.40%	9.01%	100.00%
Oct	2.82%	2.82%	9.41%	100.00%
Nov	2.68%	2.68%	5.97%	100.00%
Dec	2.83%	2.83%	5.49%	100.00%
Averages	0.79%	1.14%	6.39%	85.31%

Figures from: 06/20/2000 to: 12/28/2017

WEEKLY AVERAGE RETURNS

Week No.	BUY	SELL	Buy & Hold
1		0.45%	0.45%
2		-0.97%	-0.97%
3		-1.37%	-1.37%
4	0.42%		0.42%
5	0.69%		0.69%
6	0.90%		0.90%
7	1.03%		1.03%
8	-0.01%		-0.01%
9	0.41%		0.41%
10	0.61%		0.61%
11	0.89%		0.89%
12	0.20%		0.20%
13	0.43%		0.43%
14	1.53%		1.53%
15	-0.06%		-0.06%
16	0.68%		0.68%
17	1.24%		1.24%
18	0.57%		0.57%
19		-0.96%	-0.96%
20		-0.61%	-0.61%
21	-0.18%		-0.18%
22	1.19%		1.19%
23	-0.41%		-0.41%
24	0.55%		0.55%
25	-0.04%		-0.04%
26	0.26%		0.26%
27	-0.40%		-0.40%

Week No.	BUY	SELL	Buy & Hold
27	-0.40%		-0.40%
28	0.53%		0.53%
29	0.36%		0.36%
30	0.60%		0.60%
31		-0.73%	-0.73%
32		-0.39%	-0.39%
33	0.40%		0.40%
34	0.13%		0.13%
35	0.64%		0.64%
36	-0.21%		-0.21%
37	0.32%		0.32%
38	0.19%		0.19%
39	-1.98%		-1.98%
40	0.15%		0.15%
41	1.20%		1.20%
42	-0.46%		-0.46%
43	-0.66%		-0.66%
44	1.98%		1.98%
45	0.38%		0.38%
46	0.17%		0.17%
47	-0.23%		-0.23%
48	1.10%		1.10%
49	1.70%		1.70%
50	-0.71%		-0.71%
51	0.33%		0.33%
52	1.75%		1.75%
53	0.17%		0.17%
Averages	0.40%	-0.69%	0.26%

HISTORICAL YEARLY RETURNS

Year	Market Value Buy & Hold Strategy	Market Value Trading Strategy	Annual Returns Buy & Hold Strategy	Annual Returns Trading Strategy	Win
2000	$ 11,359	$ 11,646	14%	16%	Y
2001	$ 11,325	$ 12,039	0%	3%	Y
2002	$ 10,305	$ 11,301	-9%	-6%	Y
2003	$ 13,941	$ 14,994	35%	33%	N
2004	$ 15,649	$ 17,945	12%	20%	Y
2005	$ 16,296	$ 19,981	4%	11%	Y
2006	$ 19,077	$ 25,368	17%	27%	Y
2007	$ 25,213	$ 32,223	32%	27%	N
2008	$ 12,424	$ 17,210	-51%	-47%	Y
2009	$ 20,422	$ 27,279	64%	59%	N
2010	$ 26,751	$ 35,985	31%	32%	Y
2011	$ 22,685	$ 38,718	-15%	8%	Y
2012	$ 24,942	$ 41,439	10%	7%	N
2013	$ 29,899	$ 45,184	20%	9%	N
2014	$ 30,802	$ 47,671	3%	6%	Y
2015	$ 26,859	$ 42,748	-13%	-10%	Y
2016	$ 32,162	$ 60,551	20%	42%	Y
2017	$ 40,143	$ 76,710	25%	27%	Y
Averages	-	-	11.1%	14.6%	84.2%

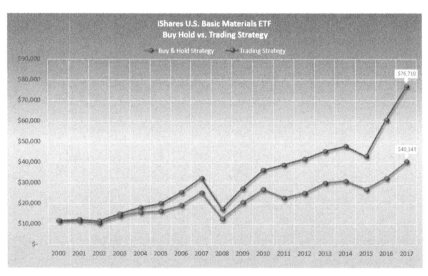

ISHARES U.S. TECHNOLOGY ETF (IYW)

SUMMARY

Ticker: IYW

Description: The investment seeks to track the investment results of the Dow Jones U.S. Technology Index. The fund generally invests at least 90% of its assets in securities of the underlying index and in depositary receipts representing securities of the underlying index. The underlying index measures the performance of the technology sector of the U.S. equity market and may include large-, mid- or small-capitalization companies, and components primarily include technology companies. The fund is non-diversified.

Data From: 5/20/2000 To: 12/28/2017		Total Return		
Winning Probability		• Buy & Hold:		66.14%
• Monthly:	80.19%	• Trading Strategy:		160.99%
• Annually:	73.68%	Trading Weeks:		
		BUY	**SELL**	
Average Annual Returns		7	50	
• Buy & Hold:	6.52%	34	30	
• Trading Strategy:	7.77%			
• Delta:	1.25%			

MONTHLY ANALYSIS

Month	Average Return Buy & Hold Strategy	Average Return Trading Strategy	Standard Dev of Month Return (Volatility)	Percentage Wins
Jan	-0.09%	0.00%	8.67%	58.82%
Feb	-1.90%	-1.03%	8.64%	52.94%
Mar	0.59%	0.59%	6.43%	100.00%
Apr	1.64%	1.64%	8.20%	100.00%
May	1.12%	1.12%	5.64%	100.00%
Jun	-1.28%	-1.28%	4.55%	100.00%
Jul	0.69%	1.08%	5.33%	33.33%
Aug	0.80%	0.99%	7.30%	61.11%
Sep	-1.84%	-1.84%	8.00%	100.00%
Oct	4.22%	4.22%	9.11%	100.00%
Nov	0.85%	0.85%	8.40%	100.00%
Dec	-0.24%	0.66%	5.68%	55.56%
Averages	0.38%	0.58%	7.29%	80.19%

Figures from: 05/19/2000 to: 12/28/2017

WEEKLY AVERAGE RETURNS

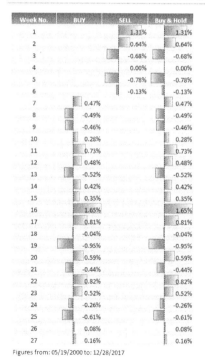

Week No.	BUY	SELL	Buy & Hold
1		1.31%	1.31%
2		0.64%	0.64%
3		-0.68%	-0.68%
4		0.00%	0.00%
5		-0.78%	-0.78%
6		-0.13%	-0.13%
7	0.47%		0.47%
8	-0.49%		-0.49%
9	-0.46%		-0.46%
10	0.28%		0.28%
11	0.73%		0.73%
12	0.48%		0.48%
13	-0.52%		-0.52%
14	0.42%		0.42%
15	0.35%		0.35%
16	1.65%		1.65%
17	0.81%		0.81%
18	-0.04%		-0.04%
19	-0.95%		-0.95%
20	0.59%		0.59%
21	-0.44%		-0.44%
22	0.82%		0.82%
23	0.52%		0.52%
24	-0.26%		-0.26%
25	-0.61%		-0.61%
26	0.08%		0.08%
27	0.16%		0.16%

Figures from: 05/19/2000 to: 12/28/2017

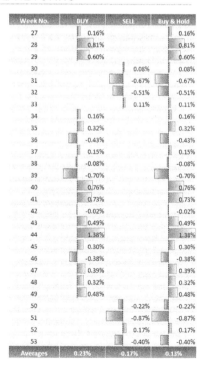

Week No.	BUY	SELL	Buy & Hold
27	0.16%		0.16%
28	0.81%		0.81%
29	0.60%		0.60%
30		0.08%	0.08%
31		-0.67%	-0.67%
32		-0.51%	-0.51%
33		0.11%	0.11%
34	0.16%		0.16%
35	0.32%		0.32%
36	-0.43%		-0.43%
37	0.15%		0.15%
38	-0.08%		-0.08%
39	-0.70%		-0.70%
40	0.76%		0.76%
41	0.73%		0.73%
42	-0.02%		-0.02%
43	0.49%		0.49%
44	1.38%		1.38%
45	0.30%		0.30%
46	-0.38%		-0.38%
47	0.39%		0.39%
48	0.32%		0.32%
49	0.48%		0.48%
50		-0.22%	-0.22%
51		-0.87%	-0.87%
52		0.17%	0.17%
53		-0.40%	-0.40%
Averages	0.23%	-0.17%	0.13%

HISTORICAL YEARLY RETURNS

Year	Market Value Buy & Hold Strategy	Market Value Trading Strategy	Annual Returns Buy & Hold Strategy	Annual Returns Trading Strategy	Win
1999	$ 10,000	$ 10,000	0%	0%	Y
2000	$ 6,794	$ 8,523	-32%	-15%	Y
2001	$ 4,847	$ 7,071	-29%	-17%	Y
2002	$ 2,961	$ 4,995	-39%	-29%	Y
2003	$ 4,420	$ 7,702	49%	54%	Y
2004	$ 4,479	$ 8,135	1%	6%	Y
2005	$ 4,603	$ 9,227	3%	13%	Y
2006	$ 5,061	$ 8,956	10%	-3%	N
2007	$ 5,819	$ 11,117	15%	24%	Y
2008	$ 3,308	$ 6,750	-43%	-39%	Y
2009	$ 5,419	$ 9,637	64%	43%	N
2010	$ 6,091	$ 11,827	12%	23%	Y
2011	$ 6,083	$ 12,080	0%	2%	Y
2012	$ 6,794	$ 10,963	12%	-9%	N
2013	$ 8,599	$ 12,678	27%	16%	N
2014	$ 10,272	$ 15,496	19%	22%	Y
2015	$ 10,650	$ 17,543	4%	13%	Y
2016	$ 12,112	$ 20,360	14%	16%	Y
2017	$ 16,614	$ 26,099	37%	28%	N
Averages	-	-	6.5%	7.8%	73.7%

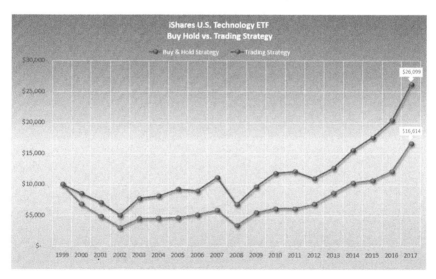

65

ISHARES U.S. TELECOMMUNICATIONS ETF (IYZ)

SUMMARY

Ticker: IYZ

Description: The investment seeks to track the investment results of the Dow Jones U.S. Select Telecommunications Index. The fund generally invests at least 90% of its assets in securities of the underlying index and in depositary receipts representing securities of the underlying index. The underlying fund measures the performance of the telecommunications sector of the U.S. equity market and may include large-, mid- or small-capitalization companies. The fund is non-diversified.

Data From: 5/26/2000 To: 12/28/2017		Total Return		
Winning Probability		• Buy & Hold:		-16.43%
• Monthly:	75.94%	• Trading Strategy:		203.25%
• Annually:	68.42%	Trading Weeks:		
		BUY		**SELL**
Average Annual Returns		6		2
• Buy & Hold:	1.74%			
• Trading Strategy:	7.30%	42		25
• Delta:	5.56%			

MONTHLY ANALYSIS

Month	Average Return Buy & Hold Strategy	Average Return Trading Strategy	Standard Dev of Month Return (Volatility)	Percentage Wins
Jan	-2.39%	0.20%	7.02%	64.71%
Feb	-1.44%	-1.33%	5.82%	82.35%
Mar	1.25%	1.25%	4.32%	100.00%
Apr	1.13%	1.13%	5.45%	100.00%
May	0.31%	0.31%	4.04%	100.00%
Jun	-0.24%	0.19%	5.24%	55.56%
Jul	-0.14%	0.00%	5.50%	44.44%
Aug	-1.51%	0.00%	3.93%	66.67%
Sep	-1.13%	0.00%	6.34%	55.56%
Oct	0.79%	1.60%	9.48%	44.44%
Nov	-0.12%	-0.12%	5.18%	100.00%
Dec	1.81%	1.81%	5.40%	100.00%
Averages	-0.14%	0.42%	5.80%	75.94%

Figures from: 05/26/2000 to: 12/28/2017

WEEKLY AVERAGE RETURNS

Week No.	BUY	SELL	Buy & Hold
1	0.26%		0.26%
2		-0.19%	-0.19%
3		-1.76%	-1.76%
4		-0.26%	-0.26%
5		-0.66%	-0.66%
6	-0.07%		-0.07%
7	0.33%		0.33%
8	-0.47%		-0.47%
9	-0.38%		-0.38%
10	0.15%		0.15%
11	0.91%		0.91%
12	0.42%		0.42%
13	-0.12%		-0.12%
14	1.85%		1.85%
15	-0.86%		-0.86%
16	0.26%		0.26%
17	1.39%		1.39%
18	0.71%		0.71%
19	-1.54%		-1.54%
20	0.44%		0.44%
21	-0.24%		-0.24%
22	0.70%		0.70%
23	0.18%		0.18%
24	0.26%		0.26%
25		-0.35%	-0.35%
26		0.35%	0.35%
27		-0.02%	-0.02%

Week No.	BUY	SELL	Buy & Hold
27		-0.02%	-0.02%
28		0.19%	0.19%
29		-0.36%	-0.36%
30		0.60%	0.60%
31		-0.31%	-0.31%
32		-1.27%	-1.27%
33		-0.13%	-0.13%
34		-0.57%	-0.57%
35		0.51%	0.51%
36		-0.32%	-0.32%
37		0.12%	0.12%
38		0.72%	0.72%
39		-1.11%	-1.11%
40		0.94%	0.94%
41		-0.89%	-0.89%
42	-0.15%		-0.15%
43	-0.41%		-0.41%
44	0.84%		0.84%
45	-1.47%		-1.47%
46	0.34%		0.34%
47	-0.54%		-0.54%
48	1.28%		1.28%
49	0.59%		0.59%
50	-0.55%		-0.55%
51	1.02%		1.02%
52	0.10%		0.10%
53	0.12%		0.12%
Averages	0.17%	-0.22%	0.01%

Figures from: 05/26/2000 to: 12/28/2017

67

Year	Market Value Buy & Hold Strategy	Market Value Trading Strategy	Annual Returns Buy & Hold Strategy	Annual Returns Trading Strategy	Win
2000	$ 7,064	$ 8,717	-29%	-13%	Y
2001	$ 5,775	$ 7,247	-18%	-17%	Y
2002	$ 3,547	$ 6,408	-39%	-12%	Y
2003	$ 4,035	$ 8,390	14%	31%	Y
2004	$ 4,772	$ 8,809	18%	5%	N
2005	$ 4,649	$ 9,158	-3%	4%	Y
2006	$ 6,164	$ 10,558	33%	15%	N
2007	$ 6,254	$ 10,138	1%	-4%	N
2008	$ 3,626	$ 10,528	-42%	4%	Y
2009	$ 4,578	$ 14,425	26%	37%	Y
2010	$ 5,524	$ 16,965	21%	18%	N
2011	$ 5,114	$ 18,981	-7%	12%	Y
2012	$ 6,068	$ 18,621	19%	-2%	N
2013	$ 7,657	$ 21,468	26%	15%	N
2014	$ 7,709	$ 22,943	1%	7%	Y
2015	$ 7,726	$ 24,987	0%	9%	Y
2016	$ 9,484	$ 31,100	23%	24%	Y
2017	$ 8,357	$ 30,325	-12%	-2%	Y
Averages	-	-	1.7%	7.3%	68.4%

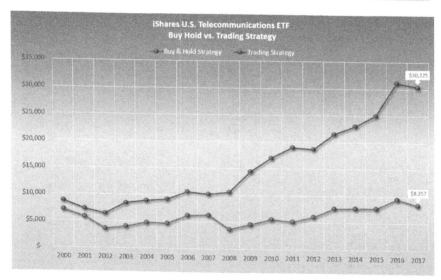

iShares U.S. Telecommunications ETF
Buy Hold vs. Trading Strategy

ISHARES U.S. UTILITIES ETF (IDU)

SUMMARY

Ticker: IDU

Description: The investment seeks to track the investment results of the Dow Jones U.S. Utilities Index. The fund generally invests at least 90% of its assets in securities of the underlying index and in depositary receipts representing securities of the underlying index. The underlying fund measures the performance of the utilities sector of the U.S. equity market and may include large-, mid- or small-capitalization companies. The fund is non-diversified.

Data From: 6/20/2000 To: 12/28/2017		Total Return		
Winning Probability		• Buy & Hold:		244.10%
• Monthly:	71.56%	• Trading Strategy:		371.52%
• Annually:	52.63%	Trading Weeks:		
		BUY		**SELL**
Average Annual Returns		6		1
• Buy & Hold:	8.33%			
• Trading Strategy:	8.85%	22		19
• Delta:	0.53%	47		35

⚠ NOTE: Due to the very low delta and the low annual winning probability, it is marginal to use the trading strategy versus the buy and hold method. Some industries do not have any seasonal trending.

MONTHLY ANALYSIS

Month	Average Return Buy & Hold Strategy	Average Return Trading Strategy	Standard Dev of Month Return (Volatility)	Percentage Wins
Jan	-0.64%	0.08%	3.88%	47.06%
Feb	-0.42%	-0.52%	4.81%	76.47%
Mar	2.53%	2.53%	3.32%	100.00%
Apr	1.82%	1.82%	2.84%	100.00%
May	0.25%	0.87%	4.28%	58.82%
Jun	0.13%	0.13%	3.86%	100.00%
Jul	-0.23%	-0.23%	5.51%	100.00%
Aug	0.88%	0.85%	4.59%	50.00%
Sep	-0.42%	0.00%	5.21%	38.89%
Oct	0.67%	0.00%	5.11%	33.33%
Nov	0.27%	0.71%	2.62%	55.56%
Dec	2.71%	2.71%	3.25%	100.00%
Averages	0.63%	0.75%	4.25%	71.56%

Figures from: 06/20/2000 to: 12/28/2017

WEEKLY AVERAGE RETURNS

Week No.	BUY	SELL	Buy & Hold		Week No.	BUY	SELL	Buy & Hold
1		-0.88%	-0.88%		27	-0.47%		-0.47%
2		-0.45%	-0.45%		28	0.08%		0.08%
3		-0.14%	-0.14%		29	-0.61%		-0.61%
4		-0.09%	-0.09%		30	-0.07%		-0.07%
5		0.63%	0.63%		31	-0.02%		-0.02%
6	-0.17%		-0.17%		32	0.32%		0.32%
7	-0.16%		-0.16%		33	0.30%		0.30%
8	0.09%		0.09%		34	0.63%		0.63%
9	-0.23%		-0.23%		35		-0.14%	-0.14%
10	0.24%		0.24%		36		-0.09%	-0.09%
11	0.38%		0.38%		37		-0.41%	-0.41%
12	0.77%		0.77%		38		0.36%	0.36%
13	0.20%		0.20%		39		-0.67%	-0.67%
14	0.68%		0.68%		40		0.39%	0.39%
15	-0.17%		-0.17%		41		-1.16%	-1.16%
16	0.87%		0.87%		42		-0.06%	-0.06%
17	0.46%		0.46%		43		-0.45%	-0.45%
18	0.44%		0.44%		44		0.45%	0.45%
19		-0.90%	-0.90%		45		-0.59%	-0.59%
20		-0.06%	-0.06%		46		-0.27%	-0.27%
21		-0.09%	-0.09%		47	0.08%		0.08%
22	0.73%		0.73%		48	0.29%		0.29%
23	-0.68%		-0.68%		49	0.34%		0.34%
24	0.75%		0.75%		50	-0.09%		-0.09%
25	-0.11%		-0.11%		51	1.18%		1.18%
26	0.01%		0.01%		52	0.87%		0.87%
27	-0.47%		-0.47%		53	-0.25%		-0.25%
					Averages	0.20%	-0.22%	0.04%

Figures from: 06/20/2000 to: 12/28/2017

70

	Market Value		Annual Returns		
Year	Buy & Hold Strategy	Trading Strategy	Buy & Hold Strategy	Trading Strategy	Win
1999	$ 10,000	$ 10,000	0%	0%	Y
2000	$ 13,122	$ 12,228	31%	22%	N
2001	$ 9,727	$ 11,333	-26%	-7%	Y
2002	$ 7,568	$ 10,927	-22%	-4%	Y
2003	$ 9,502	$ 12,086	26%	11%	N
2004	$ 11,695	$ 13,399	23%	11%	N
2005	$ 13,398	$ 15,771	15%	18%	Y
2006	$ 16,182	$ 18,194	21%	15%	N
2007	$ 18,886	$ 20,523	17%	13%	N
2008	$ 13,188	$ 20,103	-30%	-2%	Y
2009	$ 14,816	$ 23,362	12%	16%	Y
2010	$ 15,883	$ 26,670	7%	14%	Y
2011	$ 18,851	$ 27,599	19%	3%	N
2012	$ 19,068	$ 30,108	1%	9%	Y
2013	$ 21,887	$ 32,642	15%	8%	N
2014	$ 27,872	$ 38,574	27%	18%	N
2015	$ 26,524	$ 37,471	-5%	-3%	Y
2016	$ 30,889	$ 44,923	16%	20%	Y
2017	$ 34,410	$ 47,152	11%	5%	N
Averages	-	-	8.3%	8.9%	52.6%

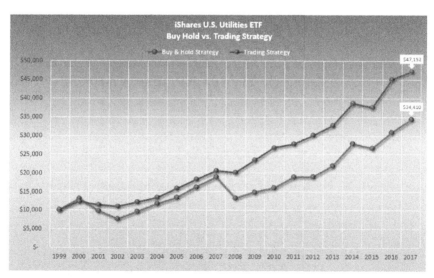

ISHARES U.S. REAL ESTATE ETF (IYR)

SUMMARY

Ticker: IYR

Description: The investment seeks to track the investment results of the Dow Jones U.S. Real Estate Index. The fund generally invests at least 90% of its assets in securities of the underlying index and in depositary receipts representing securities of the underlying index. The underlying fund measures the performance of the real estate sector of the U.S. equity market and may include large-, mid- or small-capitalization companies, and components primarily include real estate investment trusts ("REITs").

Data From: 6/20/2000 To: 12/28/2017		Total Return		
Winning Probability		• Buy & Hold:		397.92%
• Monthly:	83.41%	• Trading Strategy:		1,080.14%
• Annually:	57.89%	Trading Weeks:		
			BUY	SELL
Average Annual Returns			21	19
• Buy & Hold:	10.57%			
• Trading Strategy:	14.64%		48	38
• Delta:	4.07%			

MONTHLY ANALYSIS

Month	Average Return Buy & Hold Strategy	Average Return Trading Strategy	Standard Dev of Month Return (Volatility)	Percentage Wins
Jan	0.28%	0.28%	5.50%	100.00%
Feb	-0.61%	-0.61%	6.12%	100.00%
Mar	2.90%	2.90%	3.88%	100.00%
Apr	2.23%	2.23%	8.94%	100.00%
May	0.22%	1.35%	3.99%	52.94%
Jun	-0.06%	-0.06%	5.05%	100.00%
Jul	1.55%	1.55%	4.91%	100.00%
Aug	0.24%	0.24%	4.65%	100.00%
Sep	0.10%	0.70%	4.68%	55.56%
Oct	-0.14%	0.00%	9.43%	44.44%
Nov	0.25%	2.20%	5.98%	50.00%
Dec	4.21%	4.21%	10.40%	100.00%
Averages	0.93%	1.25%	6.48%	83.41%

Figures from: 06/19/2000 to: 12/28/2017

WEEKLY AVERAGE RETURNS

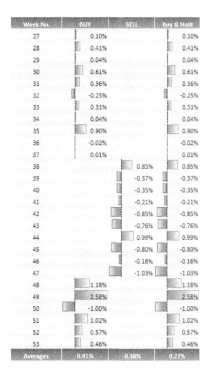

Week No.	BUY	SELL	Buy & Hold
1	-0.21%		-0.21%
2	-0.40%		-0.40%
3	0.05%		0.05%
4	0.85%		0.85%
5	0.51%		0.51%
6	-0.27%		-0.27%
7	-0.11%		-0.11%
8	0.54%		0.54%
9	-0.12%		-0.12%
10	-0.11%		-0.11%
11	1.69%		1.69%
12	1.21%		1.21%
13	-0.54%		-0.54%
14	2.21%		2.21%
15	-0.46%		-0.46%
16	1.26%		1.26%
17	1.70%		1.70%
18	0.24%		0.24%
19		-1.05%	-1.05%
20		-0.92%	-0.92%
21	-0.56%		-0.56%
22	0.66%		0.66%
23	-0.16%		-0.16%
24	0.57%		0.57%
25	-0.15%		-0.15%
26	0.76%		0.76%
27	0.10%		0.10%

Figures from: 06/19/2000 to: 12/28/2017

Week No.	BUY	SELL	Buy & Hold
27	0.10%		0.10%
28	0.41%		0.41%
29	0.04%		0.04%
30	0.61%		0.61%
31	0.36%		0.36%
32	-0.25%		-0.25%
33	0.31%		0.31%
34	0.04%		0.04%
35	0.90%		0.90%
36	-0.02%		-0.02%
37	0.01%		0.01%
38		0.85%	0.85%
39		-0.37%	-0.37%
40		-0.35%	-0.35%
41		-0.21%	-0.21%
42		-0.85%	-0.85%
43		-0.76%	-0.76%
44		0.99%	0.99%
45		-0.80%	-0.80%
46		-0.16%	-0.16%
47		-1.03%	-1.03%
48	1.18%		1.18%
49	2.58%		2.58%
50	-1.00%		-1.00%
51	1.02%		1.02%
52	0.57%		0.57%
53	0.46%		0.46%
Averages	0.41%	-0.38%	0.22%

| | Market Value | | Annual Returns | | |
Year	Buy & Hold Strategy	Trading Strategy	Buy & Hold Strategy	Trading Strategy	Win
1999	$ 10,000	$ 10,000	0%	0%	Y
2000	$ 11,227	$ 11,740	12%	17%	Y
2001	$ 12,162	$ 12,759	8%	9%	Y
2002	$ 12,581	$ 14,023	3%	10%	Y
2003	$ 17,028	$ 17,468	35%	25%	N
2004	$ 22,158	$ 21,730	30%	24%	N
2005	$ 24,142	$ 23,784	9%	9%	Y
2006	$ 32,570	$ 30,374	35%	28%	N
2007	$ 26,658	$ 28,390	-18%	-7%	Y
2008	$ 16,028	$ 39,749	-40%	40%	Y
2009	$ 20,929	$ 50,978	31%	28%	N
2010	$ 26,484	$ 64,985	27%	27%	Y
2011	$ 27,952	$ 69,450	6%	7%	Y
2012	$ 33,042	$ 92,787	18%	34%	Y
2013	$ 33,426	$ 91,466	1%	-1%	N
2014	$ 42,348	$ 106,188	27%	16%	N
2015	$ 43,032	$ 98,599	2%	-7%	N
2016	$ 46,047	$ 110,408	7%	12%	Y
2017	$ 49,792	$ 118,014	8%	7%	N
Averages	-	-	10.6%	14.6%	57.9%

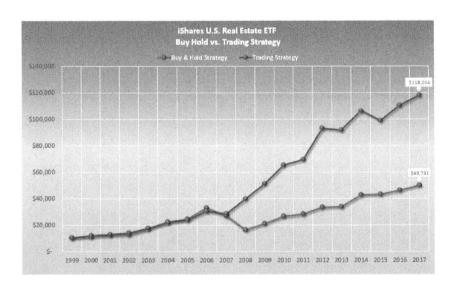

ISHARES U.S. CONSUMER GOODS ETF (IYK)

SUMMARY

Ticker: IYK

Description: The investment seeks to track the investment results of the Dow Jones U.S. Consumer Goods Index composed of U.S. equities in the consumer goods sector. The fund generally invests at least 90% of its assets in securities of the underlying index and in depositary receipts representing securities of the underlying index. The underlying index measures the performance of the consumer goods sector of the U.S. equity market. The fund may invest the remainder of its assets in certain futures, options and swap contracts, cash and cash equivalents. It is non-diversified.

Data From: 6/16/2000 To: 12/28/2017		Total Return	
Winning Probability		• Buy & Hold:	329.27%
• Monthly:	87.68%	• Trading Strategy:	469.15%
• Annually:	63.16%	Trading Weeks:	
		BUY	**SELL**
Average Annual Returns		5	1
• Buy & Hold:	8.68%	44	38
• Trading Strategy:	9.85%		
• Delta:	1.17%		

75

MONTHLY ANALYSIS

Month	Average Return Buy & Hold Strategy	Average Return Trading Strategy	Standard Dev of Month Return (Volatility)	Percentage Wins
Jan	-1.19%	-0.14%	3.35%	58.82%
Feb	1.20%	1.20%	3.51%	100.00%
Mar	1.34%	1.34%	3.10%	100.00%
Apr	1.15%	1.15%	2.30%	100.00%
May	0.80%	0.80%	3.51%	100.00%
Jun	-0.87%	-0.87%	2.56%	100.00%
Jul	0.55%	0.55%	4.09%	100.00%
Aug	0.19%	0.19%	3.10%	100.00%
Sep	-0.11%	0.69%	3.12%	61.11%
Oct	1.13%	1.12%	5.34%	33.33%
Nov	1.33%	1.33%	2.77%	100.00%
Dec	1.53%	1.53%	1.98%	100.00%
Averages	0.59%	0.74%	3.36%	87.68%

Figures from: 06/16/2000 to: 12/28/2017

WEEKLY AVERAGE RETURNS

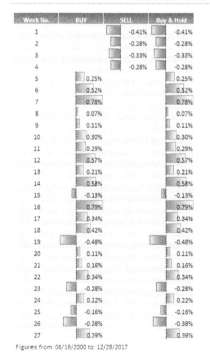

Week No.	BUY	SELL	Buy & Hold
1		-0.41%	-0.41%
2		-0.28%	-0.28%
3		-0.33%	-0.33%
4		-0.28%	-0.28%
5	0.25%		0.25%
6	0.52%		0.52%
7	0.78%		0.78%
8	0.07%		0.07%
9	0.11%		0.11%
10	0.30%		0.30%
11	0.29%		0.29%
12	0.57%		0.57%
13	0.21%		0.21%
14	0.58%		0.58%
15	-0.13%		-0.13%
16	0.79%		0.79%
17	0.34%		0.34%
18	0.42%		0.42%
19	-0.48%		-0.48%
20	0.11%		0.11%
21	0.16%		0.16%
22	0.34%		0.34%
23	-0.28%		-0.28%
24	0.22%		0.22%
25	-0.16%		-0.16%
26	-0.38%		-0.38%
27	0.39%		0.39%

Figures from: 06/16/2000 to: 12/28/2017

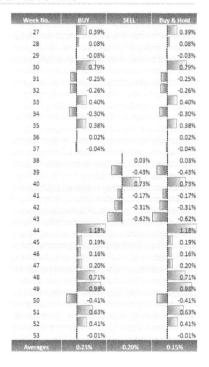

Week No.	BUY	SELL	Buy & Hold
27	0.39%		0.39%
28	0.08%		0.08%
29	-0.03%		-0.03%
30	0.79%		0.79%
31	-0.25%		-0.25%
32	-0.26%		-0.26%
33	0.40%		0.40%
34	-0.30%		-0.30%
35	0.38%		0.38%
36	0.02%		0.02%
37	-0.04%		-0.04%
38		0.03%	0.03%
39		-0.43%	-0.43%
40		0.73%	0.73%
41		-0.17%	-0.17%
42		-0.31%	-0.31%
43		-0.62%	-0.62%
44	1.18%		1.18%
45	0.19%		0.19%
46	0.16%		0.16%
47	0.20%		0.20%
48	0.71%		0.71%
49	0.98%		0.98%
50	-0.41%		-0.41%
51	0.63%		0.63%
52	0.41%		0.41%
53	-0.01%		-0.01%
Averages	0.23%	-0.20%	0.15%

| Year | Market Value | | Annual Returns | | Win |
	Buy & Hold Strategy	Trading Strategy	Buy & Hold Strategy	Trading Strategy	
1999	$ 10,000	$ 10,000	0%	0%	Y
2000	$ 10,563	$ 11,000	6%	10%	Y
2001	$ 10,734	$ 11,760	2%	7%	Y
2002	$ 10,149	$ 11,416	-5%	-3%	Y
2003	$ 12,286	$ 13,599	21%	19%	N
2004	$ 13,759	$ 15,841	12%	16%	Y
2005	$ 13,968	$ 16,970	2%	7%	Y
2006	$ 15,968	$ 18,485	14%	9%	N
2007	$ 17,429	$ 19,028	9%	3%	N
2008	$ 12,893	$ 20,899	-26%	10%	Y
2009	$ 15,901	$ 26,251	23%	26%	Y
2010	$ 18,915	$ 29,741	19%	13%	N
2011	$ 20,507	$ 30,261	8%	2%	N
2012	$ 22,968	$ 34,015	12%	12%	Y
2013	$ 29,902	$ 40,301	30%	18%	N
2014	$ 33,356	$ 46,638	12%	16%	Y
2015	$ 35,275	$ 45,084	6%	-3%	N
2016	$ 36,960	$ 49,792	5%	10%	Y
2017	$ 42,927	$ 56,915	16%	14%	N
Averages	-	-	8.7%	9.8%	63.2%

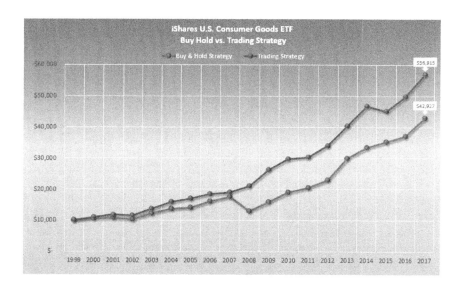

ISHARES U.S. CONSUMER SERVICES ETF (IYC)

SUMMARY

Ticker: IYC

Description: The investment seeks to track the investment results of the Dow Jones U.S. Consumer Services Index composed of U.S. equities in the consumer services sector. The fund generally invests at least 90% of its assets in securities of the underlying index and in depositary receipts representing securities of the underlying index. The underlying index measures the performance of the consumer services sector of the U.S. equity market.

Data From: 6/28/2000 To: 12/28/2017		Total Return		
Winning Probability		• Buy & Hold:		246.71%
• Monthly:	76.30%	• Trading Strategy:		414.06%
• Annually:	52.63%	Trading Weeks:		
		BUY		**SELL**
Average Annual Returns		41		19
• Buy & Hold:	8.39%			
• Trading Strategy:	9.67%			
• Delta:	1.28%			

MONTHLY ANALYSIS

Month	Average Return Buy & Hold Strategy	Average Return Trading Strategy	Standard Dev of Month Return (Volatility)	Percentage Wins
Jan	-0.37%	-0.37%	5.53%	100.00%
Feb	0.72%	0.72%	4.18%	100.00%
Mar	1.78%	1.78%	3.88%	100.00%
Apr	2.02%	2.02%	4.74%	100.00%
May	0.12%	0.18%	3.02%	52.94%
Jun	-1.59%	0.00%	3.81%	66.67%
Jul	0.30%	0.00%	4.38%	44.44%
Aug	-0.34%	0.00%	4.75%	50.00%
Sep	-0.90%	0.00%	5.68%	50.00%
Oct	1.89%	1.52%	5.92%	55.56%
Nov	2.00%	2.00%	4.73%	100.00%
Dec	1.46%	1.46%	4.59%	100.00%
Averages	0.59%	0.78%	4.71%	76.30%

Figures from: 06/28/2000 to: 12/28/2017

WEEKLY AVERAGE RETURNS

Week No.	BUY	SELL	Buy & Hold
1	0.47%		0.47%
2	0.01%		0.01%
3	-0.41%		-0.41%
4	0.27%		0.27%
5	-0.13%		-0.13%
6	0.43%		0.43%
7	0.71%		0.71%
8	-0.04%		-0.04%
9	0.24%		0.24%
10	0.43%		0.43%
11	0.87%		0.87%
12	0.71%		0.71%
13	-0.04%		-0.04%
14	1.11%		1.11%
15	-0.09%		-0.09%
16	1.06%		1.06%
17	1.03%		1.03%
18	0.49%		0.49%
19		-0.82%	-0.82%
20		-0.30%	-0.30%
21		-0.26%	-0.26%
22		0.56%	0.56%
23		-0.17%	-0.17%
24		-0.12%	-0.12%
25		-0.53%	-0.53%
26		-0.05%	-0.05%
27		0.04%	0.04%

Week No.	BUY	SELL	Buy & Hold
27		0.04%	0.04%
28		0.31%	0.31%
29		0.11%	0.11%
30		0.70%	0.70%
31		-0.63%	-0.63%
32		-0.46%	-0.46%
33		0.59%	0.59%
34		-0.48%	-0.48%
35		0.67%	0.67%
36		-0.21%	-0.21%
37		0.26%	0.26%
38		0.10%	0.10%
39		-0.53%	-0.53%
40		0.59%	0.59%
41	0.44%		0.44%
42	-0.58%		-0.58%
43	-0.03%		-0.03%
44	0.86%		0.86%
45	0.39%		0.39%
46	0.25%		0.25%
47	0.00%		0.00%
48	1.18%		1.18%
49	0.95%		0.95%
50	-0.12%		-0.12%
51	0.24%		0.24%
52	0.33%		0.33%
53	0.44%		0.44%
Averages	0.37%	-0.02%	0.20%

Figures from: 06/28/2000 to: 12/28/2017

| Year | Market Value | | Annual Returns | | Win |
	Buy & Hold Strategy	Trading Strategy	Buy & Hold Strategy	Trading Strategy	
1999	$ 10,000	$ 10,000	0%	0%	Y
2000	$ 9,376	$ 9,618	-6%	-4%	Y
2001	$ 9,376	$ 11,943	0%	24%	Y
2002	$ 7,065	$ 12,332	-25%	3%	Y
2003	$ 9,373	$ 14,464	33%	17%	N
2004	$ 10,378	$ 16,263	11%	12%	Y
2005	$ 10,136	$ 15,178	-2%	-7%	N
2006	$ 11,535	$ 16,966	14%	12%	N
2007	$ 10,647	$ 15,817	-8%	-7%	Y
2008	$ 7,391	$ 13,521	-31%	-15%	Y
2009	$ 9,804	$ 15,581	33%	15%	N
2010	$ 12,083	$ 19,745	23%	27%	Y
2011	$ 12,897	$ 24,092	7%	22%	Y
2012	$ 15,920	$ 27,171	23%	13%	N
2013	$ 22,463	$ 35,088	41%	29%	N
2014	$ 25,711	$ 38,265	14%	9%	N
2015	$ 27,276	$ 41,649	6%	9%	Y
2016	$ 28,800	$ 42,913	6%	3%	N
2017	$ 34,671	$ 51,406	20%	20%	N
Averages	-	-	8.4%	9.7%	52.6%

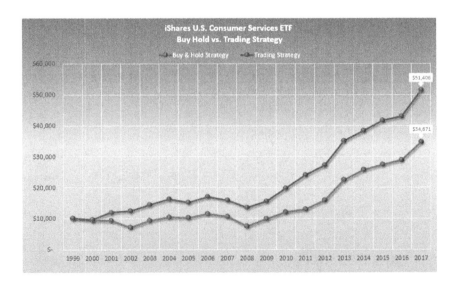

RANDGOLD RESOURCES LIMITED (GOLD)

SUMMARY

Ticker: GOLD

Description: The investment seeks to track the investment results of the Dow Jones U.S. Consumer Services Index composed of U.S. equities in the consumer services sector. The fund generally invests at least 90% of its assets in securities of the underlying index and in depositary receipts representing securities of the underlying index. The underlying index measures the performance of the consumer services sector of the U.S. equity market.

Data From: 4/01/1968 To: 12/28/2017		Total Return	
Winning Probability		• Buy & Hold:	3,298.95%
• Monthly:	87.77%	• Trading Strategy:	10,627.89%
• Annually:	60.78%	Trading Weeks:	
		BUY	SELL
Average Annual Returns		12	9
• Buy & Hold:	10.13%	45	42
• Trading Strategy:	12.95%		
• Delta:	2.82%		

MONTHLY ANALYSIS

Month	Average Return Buy & Hold Strategy	Average Return Trading Strategy	Standard Dev of Month Return (Volatility)	Percentage Wins
Jan	1.47%	1.47%	6.19%	100.00%
Feb	1.58%	2.03%	7.24%	51.02%
Mar	-0.59%	0.37%	5.18%	53.06%
Apr	0.42%	0.42%	3.96%	100.00%
May	1.40%	1.40%	6.08%	100.00%
Jun	-0.12%	-0.12%	4.91%	100.00%
Jul	0.44%	0.44%	4.48%	100.00%
Aug	0.63%	0.63%	5.11%	100.00%
Sep	1.70%	1.70%	6.48%	100.00%
Oct	-0.15%	0.43%	4.53%	60.00%
Nov	0.73%	0.81%	5.37%	88.00%
Dec	0.94%	0.94%	5.57%	100.00%
Averages	0.70%	0.88%	5.49%	87.77%

Figures from: 04/01/1968 to: 12/28/2017

WEEKLY AVERAGE RETURNS

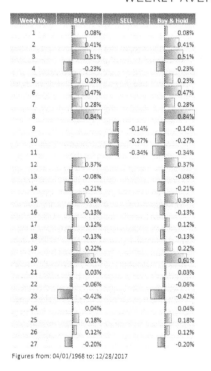

Week No.	BUY	SELL	Buy & Hold
1	0.08%		0.08%
2	0.41%		0.41%
3	0.51%		0.51%
4	-0.23%		-0.23%
5	0.23%		0.23%
6	0.47%		0.47%
7	0.28%		0.28%
8	0.84%		0.84%
9		-0.14%	-0.14%
10		-0.27%	-0.27%
11		-0.34%	-0.34%
12	0.37%		0.37%
13	-0.08%		-0.08%
14	-0.21%		-0.21%
15	0.36%		0.36%
16	-0.13%		-0.13%
17	0.12%		0.12%
18	-0.13%		-0.13%
19	0.22%		0.22%
20	0.61%		0.61%
21	0.03%		0.03%
22	-0.06%		-0.06%
23	-0.42%		-0.42%
24	0.04%		0.04%
25	0.18%		0.18%
26	0.12%		0.12%
27	-0.20%		-0.20%

Figures from: 04/01/1968 to: 12/28/2017

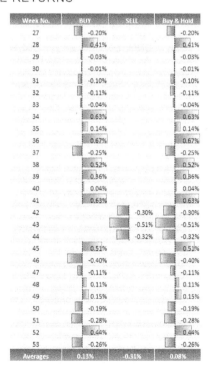

Week No.	BUY	SELL	Buy & Hold
27	-0.20%		-0.20%
28	0.41%		0.41%
29	-0.03%		-0.03%
30	-0.01%		-0.01%
31	-0.10%		-0.10%
32	-0.11%		-0.11%
33	-0.04%		-0.04%
34	0.63%		0.63%
35	0.14%		0.14%
36	0.67%		0.67%
37	-0.25%		-0.25%
38	0.52%		0.52%
39	0.36%		0.36%
40	0.04%		0.04%
41	0.63%		0.63%
42		-0.30%	-0.30%
43		-0.51%	-0.51%
44		-0.32%	-0.32%
45	0.51%		0.51%
46	-0.40%		-0.40%
47	-0.11%		-0.11%
48	0.11%		0.11%
49	0.15%		0.15%
50	-0.19%		-0.19%
51	-0.28%		-0.28%
52	0.44%		0.44%
53	-0.26%		-0.26%
Averages	0.13%	-0.31%	0.08%

HISTORICAL YEARLY RETURNS

Year	Market Value Buy & Hold Strategy	Market Value Trading Strategy	Annual Returns Buy & Hold Strategy	Annual Returns Trading Strategy	Win
1968	$ 10,520	$ 10,562	5%	6%	Y
1969	$ 9,266	$ 9,465	-12%	-10%	Y
1970	$ 9,836	$ 9,880	6%	4%	N
1971	$ 11,447	$ 11,454	16%	16%	N
1972	$ 17,026	$ 17,240	49%	51%	Y
1973	$ 29,539	$ 33,542	73%	95%	Y
1974	$ 49,342	$ 50,292	67%	50%	N
1975	$ 36,908	$ 38,410	-25%	-24%	Y
1976	$ 35,408	$ 33,918	-4%	-12%	N
1977	$ 43,579	$ 37,280	23%	10%	N
1978	$ 59,079	$ 51,595	36%	38%	Y
1979	$ 137,895	$ 129,691	133%	151%	Y
1980	$ 155,132	$ 200,697	12%	55%	Y
1981	$ 105,263	$ 150,200	-32%	-25%	Y
1982	$ 117,895	$ 199,642	12%	33%	Y
1983	$ 100,395	$ 205,777	-15%	3%	Y
1984	$ 81,316	$ 167,526	-19%	-19%	Y
1985	$ 86,053	$ 183,375	6%	9%	Y
1986	$ 102,868	$ 227,976	20%	24%	Y
1987	$ 128,026	$ 271,904	24%	19%	N
1988	$ 107,934	$ 227,183	-16%	-16%	N
1989	$ 105,526	$ 212,763	-2%	-6%	N
1990	$ 102,895	$ 220,524	-2%	4%	Y
1991	$ 93,000	$ 196,604	-10%	-11%	N
1992	$ 87,605	$ 194,516	-6%	-1%	Y
1993	$ 102,803	$ 224,420	17%	15%	N
1994	$ 100,658	$ 219,356	-2%	-2%	N
1995	$ 101,763	$ 220,629	1%	1%	N
1996	$ 97,250	$ 214,604	-4%	-3%	Y
1997	$ 76,105	$ 176,281	-22%	-18%	Y
1998	$ 75,645	$ 181,072	-1%	3%	Y
1999	$ 76,539	$ 193,419	1%	7%	Y
2000	$ 71,750	$ 190,965	-6%	-1%	Y
2001	$ 72,763	$ 195,306	1%	2%	Y
2002	$ 90,197	$ 242,793	24%	24%	Y
2003	$ 109,803	$ 300,309	22%	24%	Y
2004	$ 115,263	$ 315,003	5%	5%	N
2005	$ 135,000	$ 355,650	17%	13%	N
2006	$ 167,289	$ 403,598	24%	13%	N
2007	$ 220,132	$ 523,452	32%	30%	N
2008	$ 227,632	$ 647,026	3%	24%	Y
2009	$ 290,526	$ 882,451	28%	36%	Y
2010	$ 371,118	$ 1,110,188	28%	26%	N
2011	$ 414,342	$ 1,159,192	12%	4%	N
2012	$ 437,895	$ 1,366,735	6%	18%	Y
2013	$ 316,184	$ 957,065	-28%	-30%	N
2014	$ 312,237	$ 949,193	-1%	-1%	Y
2015	$ 279,539	$ 887,219	-10%	-7%	Y
2016	$ 305,026	$ 928,790	9%	5%	N
2017	$ 339,895	$ 1,072,789	11%	16%	Y
Averages	-	-	10.1%	13.0%	60.8%

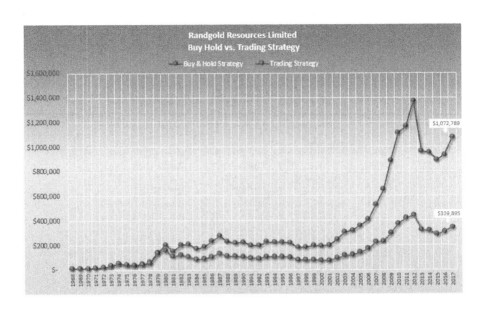

POWERSHARES DB BASE METALS (DBB)

SUMMARY

Ticker: DBB

Description: The investment seeks to track the DBIQ Optimum Yield Industrial Metals Index Excess Return™ (DBIQ-OY Industrial Metals ER™), which is intended to reflect the base metals sector. The index Commodities consist of Aluminum, Zinc and Copper – Grade A.

Data From: 1/5/2007 To: 12/28/2017		Total Return		
Winning Probability		• Buy & Hold:		-12.30%
• Monthly:	79.55%	• Trading Strategy:		238.45%
• Annually:	75.00%	Trading Weeks:		
		BUY	**SELL**	
Average Annual Returns		6	2	
• Buy & Hold:	3.48%			
• Trading Strategy:	13.08%	26	19	
• Delta:	9.60%	48	39	

MONTHLY ANALYSIS

Month	Average Return Buy & Hold Strategy	Average Return Trading Strategy	Standard Dev of Month Return (Volatility)	Percentage Wins
Jan	-1.27%	0.10%	7.63%	54.55%
Feb	2.77%	3.19%	4.57%	90.91%
Mar	0.17%	0.09%	7.02%	100.00%
Apr	1.98%	1.83%	5.11%	100.00%
May	-2.78%	0.69%	4.62%	81.82%
Jun	-0.06%	1.39%	4.22%	63.64%
Jul	2.11%	2.11%	6.21%	100.00%
Aug	-1.39%	-0.85%	4.01%	100.00%
Sep	-1.09%	-0.24%	8.12%	54.55%
Oct	-1.39%	0.00%	9.48%	36.36%
Nov	-1.19%	1.55%	5.72%	72.73%
Dec	0.04%	0.28%	5.68%	100.00%
Averages	-0.18%	0.84%	6.32%	79.55%

Figures from: 01/05/2007 to: 12/28/2017

WEEKLY AVERAGE RETURNS

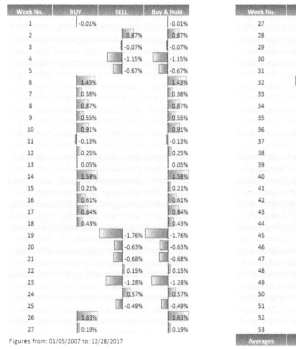

Week No.	BUY	SELL	Buy & Hold
1	-0.01%		-0.01%
2		0.87%	0.87%
3	-0.07%		-0.07%
4		-1.15%	-1.15%
5		-0.67%	-0.67%
6	1.43%		1.43%
7	0.38%		0.38%
8	0.87%		0.87%
9	0.55%		0.55%
10	0.91%		0.91%
11	-0.13%		-0.13%
12	0.25%		0.25%
13	0.05%		0.05%
14	1.58%		1.58%
15	0.21%		0.21%
16	0.61%		0.61%
17	0.84%		0.84%
18	0.43%		0.43%
19		-1.76%	-1.76%
20		-0.63%	-0.63%
21		-0.68%	-0.68%
22	0.15%		0.15%
23		-1.28%	-1.28%
24		0.57%	0.57%
25		-0.49%	-0.49%
26	1.63%		1.63%
27	0.19%		0.19%

Figures from: 01/05/2007 to: 12/28/2017

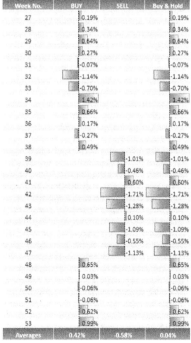

Week No.	BUY	SELL	Buy & Hold
27	0.19%		0.19%
28	0.34%		0.34%
29	0.64%		0.64%
30	0.27%		0.27%
31	-0.07%		-0.07%
32	-1.14%		-1.14%
33	-0.70%		-0.70%
34	1.42%		1.42%
35	0.66%		0.66%
36	0.17%		0.17%
37	-0.27%		-0.27%
38	0.49%		0.49%
39		-1.01%	-1.01%
40		-0.46%	-0.46%
41		0.60%	0.60%
42		-1.71%	-1.71%
43		-1.28%	-1.28%
44	0.10%		0.10%
45		-1.09%	-1.09%
46		-0.55%	-0.55%
47		-1.13%	-1.13%
48	0.65%		0.65%
49	0.03%		0.03%
50	-0.06%		-0.06%
51	-0.06%		-0.06%
52	0.62%		0.62%
53	0.99%		0.99%
Averages	0.42%	-0.58%	0.04%

HISTORICAL YEARLY RETURNS

Year	Market Value Buy & Hold Strategy	Market Value Trading Strategy	Annual Returns Buy & Hold Strategy	Annual Returns Trading Strategy	Win
2006	$ 10,000	$ 10,000	0%	0%	Y
2007	$ 9,647	$ 12,762	-4%	28%	Y
2008	$ 5,373	$ 11,096	-44%	-13%	Y
2009	$ 10,151	$ 19,567	89%	76%	N
2010	$ 11,021	$ 27,944	9%	43%	Y
2011	$ 8,414	$ 25,916	-24%	-7%	Y
2012	$ 8,698	$ 28,377	3%	9%	Y
2013	$ 7,606	$ 25,739	-13%	-9%	Y
2014	$ 7,173	$ 24,298	-6%	-6%	Y
2015	$ 5,360	$ 24,479	-25%	1%	Y
2016	$ 6,731	$ 28,937	26%	18%	N
2017	$ 8,770	$ 33,845	30%	17%	N
Averages	-	-	3.5%	13.1%	75.0%

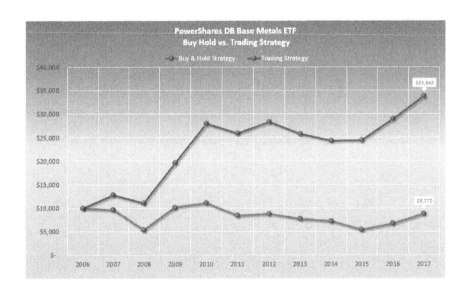

87

PROSHARES ULTRA SILVER (AGQ)

SUMMARY

Ticker: AGQ

Description: The investment seeks to provide daily investment results (before fees and expenses) that correspond to twice (200%) the daily performance of silver bullion as measured by the U.S. Dollar fixing price for delivery in London. The "Ultra" Funds seek daily results that match (before fees and expenses) two times (2x) the daily performance of a benchmark. The Ultra Funds do not seek to achieve their stated objective over a period greater than a single day.

Data From: 12/4/2008 To: 12/28/2017		Total Return		
Winning Probability		• Buy & Hold:		-26.62%
• Monthly:	69.44%	• Trading Strategy:		1,801.26%
• Annually:	81.82%	Trading Weeks:		
		BUY		**SELL**
Average Annual Returns		2		9
• Buy & Hold:	10.98%			
• Trading Strategy:	40.28%	14		19
• Delta:	29.30%	28		37

MONTHLY ANALYSIS

Month	Average Return Buy & Hold Strategy	Average Return Trading Strategy	Standard Dev of Month Return (Volatility)	Percentage Wins
Jan	4.01%	5.72%	15.26%	77.78%
Feb	5.99%	9.58%	17.02%	66.67%
Mar	-0.17%	0.24%	11.12%	44.44%
Apr	3.70%	2.87%	27.78%	100.00%
May	-2.96%	-0.29%	24.84%	66.67%
Jun	-2.84%	0.00%	21.59%	66.67%
Jul	3.87%	6.77%	13.28%	66.67%
Aug	9.35%	9.39%	18.37%	100.00%
Sep	-5.13%	4.72%	24.72%	66.67%
Oct	3.48%	0.00%	14.65%	44.44%
Nov	-1.52%	0.00%	17.66%	66.67%
Dec	-3.94%	0.00%	19.98%	66.67%
Averages	1.15%	3.25%	19.44%	69.44%

Figures from: 12/04/2008 to: 12/28/2017

WEEKLY AVERAGE RETURNS

Week No.	BUY	Sell	Buy & Hold
1		-1.88%	-1.88%
2	1.11%		1.11%
3	3.85%		3.85%
4	-0.71%		-0.71%
5	0.58%		0.58%
6	1.31%		1.31%
7	4.08%		4.08%
8	2.35%		2.35%
9		-4.05%	-4.05%
10		2.01%	2.01%
11		-0.35%	-0.35%
12		1.89%	1.89%
13		-1.78%	-1.78%
14	-1.18%		-1.18%
15	1.84%		1.84%
16	-0.79%		-0.79%
17	4.76%		4.76%
18	-0.69%		-0.69%
19		-4.30%	-4.30%
20		-0.16%	-0.16%
21		-1.04%	-1.04%
22		3.80%	3.80%
23		-4.42%	-4.42%
24		1.00%	1.00%
25		0.59%	0.59%
26		-0.33%	-0.33%
27		-1.25%	-1.25%

Week No.	BUY	Sell	Buy & Hold
27		-1.25%	-1.25%
28	1.90%		1.90%
29	1.71%		1.71%
30	0.27%		0.27%
31	-0.98%		-0.98%
32	1.57%		1.57%
33	1.77%		1.77%
34	2.89%		2.89%
35	0.78%		0.78%
36	5.59%		5.59%
37		-2.24%	-2.24%
38		1.25%	1.25%
39		-4.90%	-4.90%
40		-0.39%	-0.39%
41		1.06%	1.06%
42		0.30%	0.30%
43		-2.06%	-2.06%
44		-0.46%	-0.46%
45		2.52%	2.52%
46		-2.85%	-2.85%
47		0.51%	0.51%
48		-4.42%	-4.42%
49		1.74%	1.74%
50		-1.61%	-1.61%
51		-3.63%	-3.63%
52		1.89%	1.89%
53		0.06%	0.06%
Averages	1.52%	-0.72%	0.17%

Figures from: 12/04/2008 to: 12/28/2017

89

HISTORICAL YEARLY RETURNS

| Year | Market Value | | Annual Returns | | Win |
	Buy & Hold Strategy	Trading Strategy	Buy & Hold Strategy	Trading Strategy	
2007	$ 10,000	$ 10,000	0%	0%	Y
2008	$ 12,200	$ 10,000	22%	0%	N
2009	$ 27,072	$ 18,272	122%	83%	N
2010	$ 63,189	$ 24,068	133%	32%	N
2011	$ 44,376	$ 66,353	-30%	176%	Y
2012	$ 42,646	$ 130,042	-4%	96%	Y
2013	$ 14,162	$ 127,055	-67%	-2%	Y
2014	$ 8,957	$ 115,210	-37%	-9%	Y
2015	$ 6,178	$ 92,356	-31%	-20%	Y
2016	$ 7,502	$ 146,536	21%	59%	Y
2017	$ 6,775	$ 190,126	-10%	30%	Y
Averages	-	-	11.0%	40.3%	81.8%

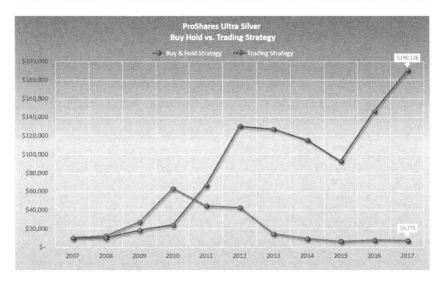

PROSHARES ULTRA FTSE EUROPE (UPV)

SUMMARY

Ticker: UPV

Description: The investment seeks daily investment results, before fees and expenses, that correspond to two times (2x) the daily performance of the FTSE Developed Europe All Cap Index. The fund invests in securities and derivatives that ProShare Advisors believes, in combination, should have similar daily return characteristics as two times (2x) the daily return of the index. The underlying index is a free float-adjusted market cap weighted index representing the performance of large, mid and small cap companies in Developed European markets, including the UK. The fund is non-diversified.

Data From: 5/7/2010 To: 12/28/2017		Total Return		
Winning Probability		• Buy & Hold:		151.40%
• Monthly:	75.00%	• Trading Strategy:		595.18%
• Annually:	77.78%	Trading Weeks:		
			BUY	SELL
Average Annual Returns			3	19
• Buy & Hold:	14.49%			
• Trading Strategy:	26.15%		27	32
• Delta:	11.66%		36	48

MONTHLY ANALYSIS

Month	Average Return Buy & Hold Strategy	Average Return Trading Strategy	Standard Dev of Month Return (Volatility)	Percentage Wins
Jan	1.25%	4.14%	5.78%	57.14%
Feb	3.78%	3.56%	9.92%	100.00%
Mar	1.54%	1.90%	4.89%	100.00%
Apr	6.18%	6.40%	7.86%	100.00%
May	-3.70%	0.26%	9.20%	62.50%
Jun	-2.31%	-0.38%	9.99%	62.50%
Jul	4.22%	4.28%	12.40%	100.00%
Aug	-5.11%	1.33%	10.22%	62.50%
Sep	0.65%	0.97%	12.25%	100.00%
Oct	6.94%	6.59%	11.72%	100.00%
Nov	-1.74%	-1.77%	7.00%	25.00%
Dec	2.44%	0.00%	7.58%	37.50%
Averages	1.18%	2.27%	9.87%	75.00%

Figures from: 05/07/2010 to: 12/28/2017

WEEKLY AVERAGE RETURNS

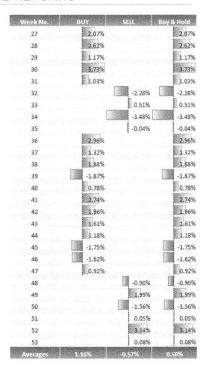

Week No.	BUY	SELL	Buy & Hold
1		-1.22%	-1.22%
2		-0.64%	-0.64%
3	2.13%		2.13%
4	0.66%		0.66%
5	1.67%		1.67%
6	0.80%		0.80%
7	2.38%		2.38%
8	1.09%		1.09%
9	1.27%		1.27%
10	1.88%		1.88%
11	0.76%		0.76%
12	0.21%		0.21%
13	-0.37%		-0.37%
14	-1.18%		-1.18%
15	0.44%		0.44%
16	0.79%		0.79%
17	2.98%		2.98%
18	1.97%		1.97%
19		-2.41%	-2.41%
20		-2.17%	-2.17%
21		-1.72%	-1.72%
22	1.28%		1.28%
23		-0.35%	-0.35%
24	0.34%		0.34%
25		-0.69%	-0.69%
26		-1.61%	-1.61%
27	2.07%		2.07%

Figures from: 05/07/2010 to: 12/28/2017

Week No.	BUY	SELL	Buy & Hold
27	2.07%		2.07%
28	2.62%		2.62%
29	1.17%		1.17%
30	3.73%		3.73%
31	1.03%		1.03%
32		-2.28%	-2.28%
33		0.51%	0.51%
34		-3.48%	-3.48%
35		-0.04%	-0.04%
36	2.96%		2.96%
37	1.32%		1.32%
38	1.88%		1.88%
39	-1.87%		-1.87%
40	0.78%		0.78%
41	2.74%		2.74%
42	1.96%		1.96%
43	1.61%		1.61%
44	1.18%		1.18%
45	-1.75%		-1.75%
46	-1.62%		-1.62%
47	0.92%		0.92%
48		-0.90%	-0.90%
49		1.99%	1.99%
50		-1.56%	-1.56%
51		0.05%	0.05%
52		3.14%	3.14%
53		0.08%	0.08%
Averages	1.16%	-0.57%	0.50%

HISTORICAL YEARLY RETURNS

| Year | Market Value | | Annual Returns | | Win |
	Buy & Hold Strategy	Trading Strategy	Buy & Hold Strategy	Trading Strategy	
2009	$ 10,000	$ 10,000	0%	0%	Y
2010	$ 14,535	$ 15,527	45%	55%	Y
2011	$ 10,130	$ 19,452	-30%	25%	Y
2012	$ 14,022	$ 25,446	38%	31%	N
2013	$ 20,445	$ 40,605	46%	60%	Y
2014	$ 19,278	$ 36,172	-6%	-11%	N
2015	$ 17,261	$ 43,110	-10%	19%	Y
2016	$ 15,565	$ 48,000	-10%	11%	Y
2017	$ 24,465	$ 69,518	57%	45%	N
Averages	-	-	14.5%	26.2%	77.8%

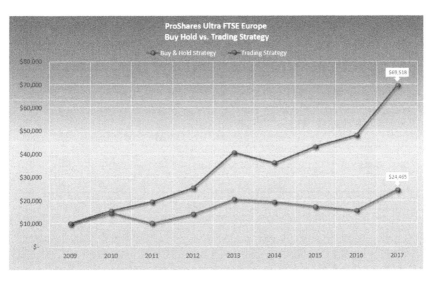

93

PROSHARES ULTRA MSCI EAFE (EFO)

SUMMARY

Ticker: EFO

Description: The investment seeks daily investment results, before fees and expenses, that correspond to two times (2x) the daily performance of the MSCI EAFE Index®. The fund invests in securities and derivatives that ProShare Advisors believes, in combination, should have similar daily return characteristics as two times (2x) the daily return of the index. The index includes 85% of free float-adjusted, market capitalization in each industry group in developed market countries, excluding the U.S. and Canada. The fund is non-diversified.

Data From: 6/04/2009 To: 12/28/2017		Total Return		
Winning Probability		• Buy & Hold:		132.49%
• Monthly:	81.55%	• Trading Strategy:		513.91%
• Annually:	80.00%	Trading Weeks:		
		BUY	SELL	
Average Annual Returns		3	19	
• Buy & Hold:	11.32%			
• Trading Strategy:	21.84%	23	32	
• Delta:	10.52%	36	49	

MONTHLY ANALYSIS

Month	Average Return Buy & Hold Strategy	Average Return Trading Strategy	Standard Dev of Month Return (Volatility)	Percentage Wins
Jan	-1.41%	2.92%	6.52%	50.00%
Feb	3.35%	3.21%	9.23%	100.00%
Mar	2.02%	2.13%	6.30%	100.00%
Apr	4.02%	4.14%	7.32%	100.00%
May	-7.19%	0.43%	10.23%	75.00%
Jun	-0.61%	-0.85%	7.94%	88.89%
Jul	5.89%	5.83%	9.54%	100.00%
Aug	-4.63%	1.15%	8.89%	55.56%
Sep	1.57%	1.73%	11.68%	100.00%
Oct	6.28%	6.12%	9.61%	100.00%
Nov	0.25%	-1.29%	4.62%	66.67%
Dec	1.65%	0.00%	6.39%	44.44%
Averages	0.93%	2.13%	9.04%	81.55%

Figures from: 06/04/2009 to: 12/28/2017

WEEKLY AVERAGE RETURNS

Week No.	BUY	SELL	Buy & Hold
1		-0.90%	-0.90%
2		-0.74%	-0.74%
3	1.37%		1.37%
4	-1.43%		-1.43%
5	1.47%		1.47%
6	0.23%		0.23%
7	0.70%		0.70%
8	1.17%		1.17%
9	0.44%		0.44%
10	2.75%		2.75%
11	0.24%		0.24%
12	0.02%		0.02%
13	-1.03%		-1.03%
14	-0.16%		-0.16%
15	-0.19%		-0.19%
16	0.87%		0.87%
17	3.91%		3.91%
18	0.14%		0.14%
19		-4.53%	-4.53%
20		-2.24%	-2.24%
21		-1.80%	-1.80%
22		0.64%	0.64%
23	-0.46%		-0.46%
24	1.72%		1.72%
25	-0.03%		-0.03%
26	-0.12%		-0.12%
27	1.04%		1.04%

Figures from: 06/04/2009 to: 12/28/2017

Week No.	BUY	SELL	Buy & Hold
27	1.04%		1.04%
28	2.00%		2.00%
29	1.47%		1.47%
30	3.70%		3.70%
31	1.34%		1.34%
32		-2.60%	-2.60%
33		0.77%	0.77%
34		-1.73%	-1.73%
35		0.69%	0.69%
36	1.58%		1.58%
37	2.51%		2.51%
38	1.60%		1.60%
39	-1.87%		-1.87%
40	-0.57%		-0.57%
41	3.26%		3.26%
42	1.25%		1.25%
43	0.95%		0.95%
44	0.16%		0.16%
45	-0.04%		-0.04%
46	-1.00%		-1.00%
47	0.92%		0.92%
48	-1.01%		-1.01%
49		0.47%	0.47%
50		-1.34%	-1.34%
51		0.50%	0.50%
52		0.32%	0.32%
53		0.00%	0.00%
Averages	0.77%	-0.80%	0.33%

HISTORICAL YEARLY RETURNS

| Year | Market Value | | Annual Returns | | Win |
	Buy & Hold Strategy	Trading Strategy	Buy & Hold Strategy	Trading Strategy	
2008	$ 10,000	$ 10,000	0%	0%	Y
2009	$ 13,724	$ 12,177	37%	22%	N
2010	$ 14,493	$ 15,258	6%	25%	Y
2011	$ 10,235	$ 14,649	-29%	-4%	Y
2012	$ 13,357	$ 21,909	31%	50%	Y
2013	$ 18,540	$ 32,625	39%	49%	Y
2014	$ 16,807	$ 30,072	-9%	-8%	Y
2015	$ 15,978	$ 44,554	-5%	48%	Y
2016	$ 15,263	$ 46,347	-4%	4%	Y
2017	$ 22,764	$ 61,391	49%	32%	N
Averages	-	-	**11.3%**	**21.8%**	**80.0%**

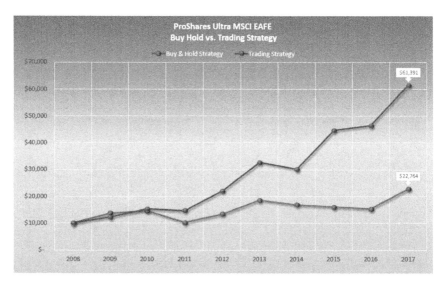

PROSHARES ULTRA MSCI JAPAN (EZJ)

SUMMARY

Ticker: EZJ

Description: The investment seeks daily investment results, before fees and expenses, that correspond to two times (2x) the daily performance of the MSCI Japan Index®. The fund invests in securities and derivatives that ProShare Advisors believes, in combination, should have similar daily return characteristics as two times (2x) the daily return of the index. The index includes 85% of free-float adjusted, market capitalization in each industry group in Japan. The fund is non-diversified.

Data From: 6/5/2009 To: 12/28/2017		Total Return		
Winning Probability		• Buy & Hold:		128.11%
• Monthly:	84.47%	• Trading Strategy:		397.38%
• Annually:	80.00%	Trading Weeks:		
			BUY	SELL
Average Annual Returns			6	19
• Buy & Hold:	10.70%			
• Trading Strategy:	20.05%		23	32
• Delta:	9.35%		36	52

MONTHLY ANALYSIS

Month	Average Return Buy & Hold Strategy	Average Return Trading Strategy	Standard Dev of Month Return (Volatility)	Percentage Wins
Jan	-1.63%	0.04%	5.92%	62.50%
Feb	4.36%	4.10%	6.44%	87.50%
Mar	1.16%	0.96%	9.73%	100.00%
Apr	2.77%	2.70%	10.40%	100.00%
May	-4.50%	1.15%	9.56%	50.00%
Jun	4.14%	3.51%	7.99%	88.89%
Jul	1.65%	1.77%	6.12%	100.00%
Aug	-5.50%	0.12%	6.56%	77.78%
Sep	1.50%	1.56%	6.41%	100.00%
Oct	2.65%	3.11%	6.66%	100.00%
Nov	0.65%	0.76%	4.79%	100.00%
Dec	1.13%	0.03%	6.80%	44.44%
Averages	0.70%	1.65%	7.78%	84.47%

WEEKLY AVERAGE RETURNS

Week No.	BUY	SELL	Buy & Hold
1		-0.46%	-0.46%
2		0.12%	0.12%
3		1.90%	1.90%
4		-0.96%	-0.96%
5		-0.19%	-0.19%
6	0.84%		0.84%
7	-0.38%		-0.38%
8	1.35%		1.35%
9	1.22%		1.22%
10	2.62%		2.62%
11	-0.55%		-0.55%
12	0.76%		0.76%
13	-0.20%		-0.20%
14	-0.50%		-0.50%
15	-0.39%		-0.39%
16	2.04%		2.04%
17	2.69%		2.69%
18	-1.30%		-1.30%
19		-1.76%	-1.76%
20		-1.50%	-1.50%
21		-2.47%	-2.47%
22		-0.25%	-0.25%
23	-0.51%		-0.51%
24	0.78%		0.78%
25	1.13%		1.13%
26	2.60%		2.60%
27	1.41%		1.41%
28	-0.14%		-0.14%
29	1.05%		1.05%
30	0.70%		0.70%
31	2.66%		2.66%
32		-2.73%	-2.73%
33		0.27%	0.27%
34		-2.23%	-2.23%
35		0.80%	0.80%
36	-0.26%		-0.26%
37	0.92%		0.92%
38	-0.16%		-0.16%
39	0.73%		0.73%
40	-0.42%		-0.42%
41	1.93%		1.93%
42	0.21%		0.21%
43	0.44%		0.44%
44	1.58%		1.58%
45	-0.67%		-0.67%
46	0.77%		0.77%
47	-0.03%		-0.03%
48	-0.87%		-0.87%
49	3.23%		3.23%
50	-0.62%		-0.62%
51	0.66%		0.66%
52		1.38%	1.38%
53		-0.38%	-0.38%
Averages	0.67%	-0.57%	0.34%

Figures from: 06/05/2009 to: 12/28/2017

HISTORICAL YEARLY RETURNS

| | Market Value | | Annual Returns | | |
Year	Buy & Hold Strategy	Trading Strategy	Buy & Hold Strategy	Trading Strategy	Win
2008	$ 10,000	$ 10,000	0%	0%	Y
2009	$ 11,262	$ 10,466	13%	5%	N
2010	$ 13,088	$ 14,407	16%	38%	Y
2011	$ 9,152	$ 13,366	-30%	-7%	Y
2012	$ 9,990	$ 15,119	9%	13%	Y
2013	$ 15,230	$ 29,913	52%	98%	Y
2014	$ 14,041	$ 30,017	-8%	0%	Y
2015	$ 15,572	$ 36,406	11%	21%	Y
2016	$ 15,936	$ 38,453	2%	6%	Y
2017	$ 22,506	$ 48,923	41%	27%	N
Averages	-	-	10.7%	20.1%	80.0%

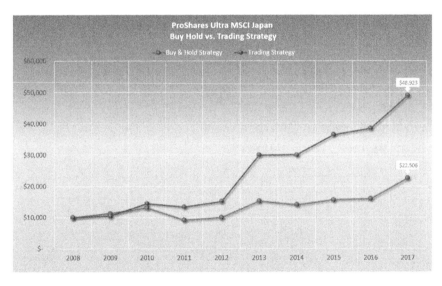

PROSHARES ULTRA FTSE CHINA 50 (XPP)

SUMMARY

Ticker: XPP

Description: The investment seeks daily investment results, before fees and expenses, that correspond to two times (2x) the daily performance of the FTSE China 50 IndexÂ®. The fund invests in securities and derivatives that ProShare Advisors believes, in combination, should have similar daily return characteristics as two times (2x) the daily return of the index. The index consists of 50 of the largest and most liquid Chinese stocks listed and traded on the Stock Exchange of Hong Kong. The fund is non-diversified.

Data From: 6/4/2009 To: 12/28/2017		Total Return		
Winning Probability		• Buy & Hold:		38.73%
• Monthly:	85.44%	• Trading Strategy:		858.67%
• Annually:	90.00%	Trading Weeks:		
		BUY		SELL
Average Annual Returns		7		19
• Buy & Hold:	6.15%			
• Trading Strategy:	27.29%	23		32
• Delta:	21.14%	36		50

MONTHLY ANALYSIS

Month	Average Return Buy & Hold Strategy	Average Return Trading Strategy	Standard Dev of Month Return (Volatility)	Percentage Wins
Jan	-5.55%	0.00%	12.23%	75.00%
Feb	1.20%	3.69%	7.58%	50.00%
Mar	2.12%	1.95%	10.98%	100.00%
Apr	2.67%	2.43%	11.72%	100.00%
May	-4.76%	0.45%	10.76%	75.00%
Jun	-1.23%	-1.35%	8.84%	88.89%
Jul	5.01%	5.41%	12.35%	100.00%
Aug	-7.73%	0.41%	10.70%	66.67%
Sep	0.68%	0.56%	15.59%	100.00%
Oct	11.55%	11.34%	13.76%	100.00%
Nov	0.93%	0.85%	6.44%	100.00%
Dec	-1.63%	2.33%	11.59%	66.67%
Averages	0.27%	2.34%	12.08%	85.44%

Figures from: 06/04/2009 to: 12/28/2017

WEEKLY AVERAGE RETURNS

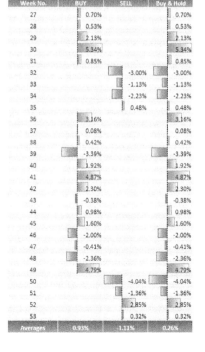

Week No.	BUY	SELL	Buy & Hold
1		-0.51%	-0.51%
2		0.34%	0.34%
3		-0.79%	-0.79%
4		-2.09%	-2.09%
5		0.31%	0.31%
6		-1.50%	-1.50%
7	3.46%		3.46%
8	-0.11%		-0.11%
9	0.80%		0.80%
10	2.24%		2.24%
11	-1.10%		-1.10%
12	0.08%		0.08%
13	-0.22%		-0.22%
14	2.57%		2.57%
15	3.58%		3.58%
16	0.27%		0.27%
17	2.04%		2.04%
18	-2.36%		-2.36%
19		-4.30%	-4.30%
20		-2.18%	-2.18%
21		-0.48%	-0.48%
22		-0.14%	-0.14%
23	-1.30%		-1.30%
24	1.57%		1.57%
25	-2.99%		-2.99%
26	2.78%		2.78%
27	0.70%		0.70%

Week No.	BUY	SELL	Buy & Hold
27	0.70%		0.70%
28	0.53%		0.53%
29	2.13%		2.13%
30	5.34%		5.34%
31	0.85%		0.85%
32		-3.00%	-3.00%
33		-1.13%	-1.13%
34		-2.23%	-2.23%
35	0.48%		0.48%
36	3.16%		3.16%
37	0.08%		0.08%
38	0.42%		0.42%
39	-3.39%		-3.39%
40	1.92%		1.92%
41	4.87%		4.87%
42	2.30%		2.30%
43	-0.38%		-0.38%
44	0.98%		0.98%
45	1.60%		1.60%
46	-2.00%		-2.00%
47	-0.41%		-0.41%
48	-2.36%		-2.36%
49	4.79%		4.79%
50		-4.04%	-4.04%
51		-1.36%	-1.36%
52		2.85%	2.85%
53	0.32%		0.32%
Averages	0.93%	-1.11%	0.26%

Figures from: 06/04/2009 to: 12/28/2017

| Year | Market Value | | Annual Returns | | Win |
	Buy & Hold Strategy	Trading Strategy	Buy & Hold Strategy	Trading Strategy	
2008	$ 10,000	$ 10,000	0%	0%	Y
2009	$ 12,237	$ 14,966	22%	50%	Y
2010	$ 12,243	$ 24,059	0%	61%	Y
2011	$ 7,748	$ 23,220	-37%	-3%	Y
2012	$ 9,615	$ 33,318	24%	43%	Y
2013	$ 9,725	$ 37,944	1%	14%	Y
2014	$ 10,833	$ 51,583	11%	36%	Y
2015	$ 8,228	$ 55,335	-24%	7%	Y
2016	$ 8,114	$ 83,028	-1%	50%	Y
2017	$ 13,354	$ 95,729	65%	15%	N
Averages	-	-	6.1%	27.3%	90.0%

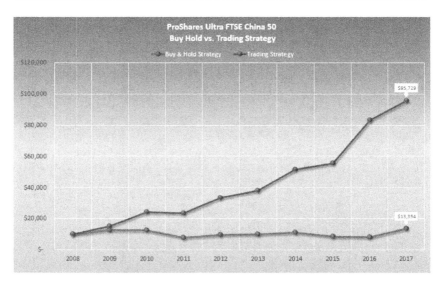

PROSHARES ULTRA MSCI EMERGING MARKETS (EET)

SUMMARY

Ticker: EET

Description: The investment seeks daily investment results, before fees and expenses, that correspond to two times (2x) the daily performance of the MSCI Emerging Markets Index®. The fund invests in securities and derivatives that ProShare Advisors believes, in combination, should have similar daily return characteristics as two times (2x) the daily return of the index. The index includes 85% of free float-adjusted market capitalization in each industry group in emerging market countries. The fund is non-diversified.

Data From: 6/4/2009 To: 12/28/2017		Total Return	
Winning Probability		• Buy & Hold:	57.25%
• Monthly:	86.41%	• Trading Strategy:	570.97%
• Annually:	80.00%	Trading Weeks:	
		BUY	SELL
Average Annual Returns		5	19
• Buy & Hold:	9.01%	23	32
• Trading Strategy:	23.58%	36	50
• Delta:	14.58%		

MONTHLY ANALYSIS

Month	Average Return Buy & Hold Strategy	Average Return Trading Strategy	Standard Dev of Month Return (Volatility)	Percentage Wins
Jan	-3.56%	-1.17%	10.78%	62.50%
Feb	1.48%	1.63%	6.16%	100.00%
Mar	6.14%	6.01%	9.90%	100.00%
Apr	1.18%	1.28%	5.75%	100.00%
May	-8.45%	0.15%	9.27%	75.00%
Jun	0.26%	0.12%	8.52%	88.89%
Jul	4.27%	4.60%	10.55%	100.00%
Aug	-6.56%	0.91%	8.34%	66.67%
Sep	2.64%	2.41%	17.63%	100.00%
Oct	7.00%	6.96%	12.85%	100.00%
Nov	-1.83%	-1.84%	6.75%	100.00%
Dec	0.68%	1.02%	7.49%	44.44%
Averages	0.27%	1.84%	10.78%	86.41%

Figures from: 06/04/2009 to: 12/26/2017

WEEKLY AVERAGE RETURNS

Week No.	BUY	SELL	Buy & Hold
1		0.49%	0.49%
2		0.33%	0.33%
3		0.11%	0.11%
4		1.88%	1.88%
5	0.67%		0.67%
6	0.27%		0.27%
7	2.40%		2.40%
8	0.37%		0.37%
9	0.48%		0.48%
10	3.46%		3.46%
11	0.39%		0.39%
12	0.11%		0.11%
13	0.21%		0.21%
14	2.40%		2.40%
15	0.78%		0.78%
16	0.48%		0.48%
17	2.44%		2.44%
18	0.42%		0.42%
19		4.51%	4.51%
20		2.27%	2.27%
21		2.66%	2.66%
22		0.11%	0.11%
23	0.19%		0.19%
24	1.29%		1.29%
25	1.41%		1.41%
26	3.20%		3.20%
27	1.34%		1.34%

Figures from: 06/04/2009 to: 12/26/2017

Week No.	BUY	SELL	Buy & Hold
27	1.34%		1.34%
28	1.98%		1.98%
29	1.91%		1.91%
30	2.63%		2.63%
31	0.80%		0.80%
32		-3.11%	-3.11%
33		-0.47%	-0.47%
34		-1.26%	-1.26%
35		1.16%	1.16%
36	3.33%		3.33%
37	0.41%		0.41%
38	0.83%		0.83%
39	-3.18%		-3.18%
40	2.16%		2.16%
41	3.73%		3.73%
42	0.90%		0.90%
43	-0.27%		-0.27%
44	-0.85%		-0.85%
45	-0.63%		-0.63%
46	-2.82%		-2.82%
47	0.44%		0.44%
48	-2.92%		-2.92%
49	3.33%		3.33%
50		-2.97%	-2.97%
51		-0.05%	-0.05%
52		3.42%	3.42%
53		0.77%	0.77%
Averages	0.77%	-0.89%	0.29%

HISTORICAL YEARLY RETURNS

Year	Market Value Buy & Hold Strategy	Market Value Trading Strategy	Annual Returns Buy & Hold Strategy	Annual Returns Trading Strategy	Win
2008	$ 10,000	$ 10,000	0%	0%	Y
2009	$ 14,761	$ 15,071	48%	51%	Y
2010	$ 18,018	$ 26,408	22%	75%	Y
2011	$ 11,123	$ 26,938	-38%	2%	Y
2012	$ 13,919	$ 35,205	25%	31%	Y
2013	$ 12,658	$ 38,278	-9%	9%	Y
2014	$ 11,591	$ 39,733	-8%	4%	Y
2015	$ 7,938	$ 35,394	-32%	-11%	Y
2016	$ 8,924	$ 51,938	12%	47%	Y
2017	$ 15,180	$ 66,916	70%	29%	N
Averages	-	-	9.0%	23.6%	80.0%

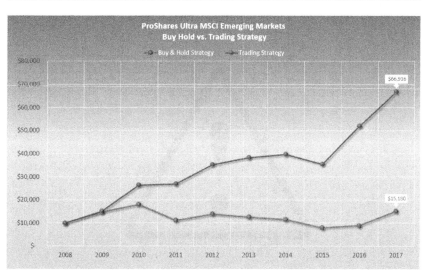

WARNING HIGH RISK HIGH RETURN ETF'S

Beyond this point are highly volatile ETF's and stocks that produce very high returns but do come with high risk. Study the historic volatility graphs and charts in the research before entering in to these positions.

DIREXION DAILY HEALTHCARE BULL 3X SHARES (CURE)

SUMMARY

Ticker: CURE

Description: The investment seeks daily investment results, before fees and expenses, of 300% of the performance of the Health Care Select Sector Index. The fund creates long positions by investing at least 80% of its assets in the securities that comprise the Health Care Select Sector Index and/or financial instruments that provide leveraged and unleveraged exposure to the index. These financial instruments include: futures contracts; options on securities, indices and futures contracts; equity caps, floors and collars; swap agreements; forward contracts; short positions; reverse repurchase agreements; exchange-traded funds; etc. It is non-diversified.

Data From: 6/15/2011 To: 12/28/2017		Total Return	
Winning Probability		• Buy & Hold:	893.81%
• Monthly:	94.94%	• Trading Strategy:	1,874.55%
• Annually:	87.50%	Trading Weeks:	
		BUY	SELL
Average Annual Returns		35	31
• Buy & Hold:	43.56%		
• Trading Strategy:	54.89%		
• Delta:	11.33%		

MONTHLY ANALYSIS

Month	Average Return Buy & Hold Strategy	Average Return Trading Strategy	Standard Dev of Month Return (Volatility)	Percentage Wins
Jan	2.15%	2.15%	11.95%	100.00%
Feb	9.05%	9.05%	11.26%	100.00%
Mar	4.05%	4.05%	9.06%	100.00%
Apr	1.05%	1.05%	4.49%	100.00%
May	3.31%	3.31%	7.29%	100.00%
Jun	4.20%	4.20%	6.48%	100.00%
Jul	3.87%	5.15%	11.53%	71.43%
Aug	-4.29%	2.59%	12.83%	71.43%
Sep	-0.50%	-0.50%	8.23%	100.00%
Oct	7.52%	7.52%	17.58%	100.00%
Nov	4.76%	4.76%	6.72%	100.00%
Dec	1.27%	1.27%	4.27%	100.00%
Averages	3.04%	3.72%	9.95%	94.94%

Figures from: 06/15/2011 to: 12/28/2017

WEEKLY AVERAGE RETURNS

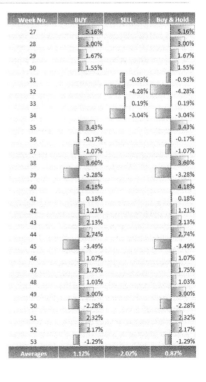

Week No.	BUY	SELL	Buy & Hold
1	1.67%		1.67%
2	1.84%		1.84%
3	0.47%		0.47%
4	0.74%		0.74%
5	1.27%		1.27%
6	0.40%		0.40%
7	4.26%		4.26%
8	1.53%		1.53%
9	1.96%		1.96%
10	1.57%		1.57%
11	-0.24%		-0.24%
12	-0.39%		-0.39%
13	1.08%		1.08%
14	-0.76%		-0.76%
15	0.94%		0.94%
16	2.47%		2.47%
17	2.42%		2.42%
18	-2.12%		-2.12%
19	-0.32%		-0.32%
20	-0.99%		-0.99%
21	1.23%		1.23%
22	1.73%		1.73%
23	2.16%		2.16%
24	1.03%		1.03%
25	1.19%		1.19%
26	0.49%		0.49%
27	5.16%		5.16%

Figures from: 06/15/2011 to: 12/28/2017

Week No.	BUY	SELL	Buy & Hold
27	5.16%		5.16%
28	3.00%		3.00%
29	1.67%		1.67%
30	1.55%		1.55%
31		-0.93%	-0.93%
32		-4.28%	-4.28%
33		0.19%	0.19%
34		-3.04%	-3.04%
35	3.43%		3.43%
36	-0.17%		-0.17%
37	-1.07%		-1.07%
38	3.60%		3.60%
39	-3.28%		-3.28%
40	4.18%		4.18%
41	0.18%		0.18%
42	1.21%		1.21%
43	2.13%		2.13%
44	2.74%		2.74%
45	-3.49%		-3.49%
46	1.07%		1.07%
47	1.75%		1.75%
48	1.03%		1.03%
49	3.00%		3.00%
50	-2.28%		-2.28%
51	2.32%		2.32%
52	2.17%		2.17%
53	-1.29%		-1.29%
Averages	1.12%	-2.02%	0.87%

HISTORICAL YEARLY RETURNS

Year	Market Value		Annual Returns		Win
	Buy & Hold Strategy	Trading Strategy	Buy & Hold Strategy	Trading Strategy	
2010	$ 10,000	$ 10,000	0%	0%	Y
2011	$ 9,031	$ 13,941	-10%	39%	Y
2012	$ 13,621	$ 21,215	51%	52%	Y
2013	$ 36,053	$ 61,034	165%	188%	Y
2014	$ 64,881	$ 104,480	80%	71%	N
2015	$ 69,696	$ 129,107	7%	24%	Y
2016	$ 57,531	$ 109,522	-17%	-15%	Y
2017	$ 99,381	$ 197,455	73%	80%	Y
Averages	-	-	43.6%	54.9%	87.5%

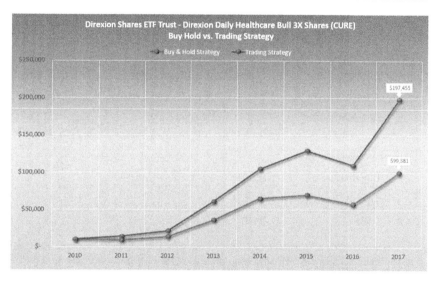

Direxion Shares ETF Trust - Direxion Daily Healthcare Bull 3X Shares (CURE) Buy Hold vs. Trading Strategy

DIREXION DAILY S&P500® BULL 3X SHARES (SPXL)

SUMMARY

Ticker: SPXL

Description: The investment seeks daily investment results, before fees and expenses, of 300% of the performance of the S&P 500® Index. The fund creates long positions by investing at least 80% of its assets in the securities that comprise the S&P 500® Index and/or financial instruments that provide leveraged and unleveraged exposure to the index. These financial instruments include: futures contracts; options on securities, indices and futures contracts; equity caps, floors and collars; swap agreements; forward contracts; short positions; reverse repurchase agreements; exchange-traded funds; and other financial instruments. It is non-diversified.

Data From: 1/2/2009 To: 12/28/2017		Total Return		
Winning Probability		• Buy & Hold:		1,537.13%
• Monthly:	86.11%	• Trading Strategy:		4,422.34%
• Annually:	70.00%	Trading Weeks:		
		BUY		**SELL**
Average Annual Returns		21		19
• Buy & Hold:	37.19%			
• Trading Strategy:	49.98%	35		31
• Delta:	12.78%			

⚠ NOTE: This is an ETF that emulates the S&P500 and on years that end in 7 or 8 should use pattern 2 on page 21-22 table 9.

MONTHLY ANALYSIS

Month	Average Return Buy & Hold Strategy	Average Return Trading Strategy	Standard Dev of Month Return (Volatility)	Percentage Wins
Jan	-5.78%	-5.78%	13.12%	100.00%
Feb	3.87%	3.87%	14.69%	100.00%
Mar	9.06%	9.06%	13.08%	100.00%
Apr	4.55%	4.55%	8.13%	100.00%
May	-1.53%	1.68%	13.24%	66.67%
Jun	-1.15%	-1.15%	9.44%	100.00%
Jul	6.92%	6.94%	11.31%	100.00%
Aug	-4.90%	-4.46%	12.63%	77.78%
Sep	3.82%	0.56%	12.02%	44.44%
Oct	10.97%	6.00%	16.78%	44.44%
Nov	5.90%	5.90%	6.62%	100.00%
Dec	3.87%	3.87%	6.21%	100.00%
Averages	2.97%	2.59%	12.32%	86.11%

Figures from: 01/02/2009 to: 12/28/2017

WEEKLY AVERAGE RETURNS

Week No.	BUY	SELL	Buy & Hold		Week No.	BUY	SELL	Buy & Hold
1	0.64%		0.64%		27	1.56%		1.56%
2	-1.00%		-1.00%		28	3.02%		3.02%
3	-0.11%		-0.11%		29	2.45%		2.45%
4	-0.32%		-0.32%		30	3.39%		3.39%
5	0.00%		0.00%		31		-0.95%	-0.95%
6	3.22%		3.22%		32		-2.89%	-2.89%
7	1.89%		1.89%		33		-0.40%	-0.40%
8	0.36%		0.36%		34		-2.18%	-2.18%
9	0.64%		0.64%		35	3.10%		3.10%
10	1.48%		1.48%		36	1.12%		1.12%
11	4.64%		4.64%		37	0.90%		0.90%
12	0.81%		0.81%		38	2.69%		2.69%
13	-0.47%		-0.47%		39	-3.16%		-3.16%
14	2.64%		2.64%		40	0.21%		0.21%
15	0.26%		0.26%		41	3.14%		3.14%
16	1.57%		1.57%		42	2.17%		2.17%
17	4.43%		4.43%		43	2.52%		2.52%
18	0.49%		0.49%		44	0.62%		0.62%
19		-2.83%	-2.83%		45	0.79%		0.79%
20		-2.77%	-2.77%		46	-0.96%		-0.96%
21	-2.09%		-2.09%		47	0.84%		0.84%
22	0.75%		0.75%		48	-0.58%		-0.58%
23	0.15%		0.15%		49	3.64%		3.64%
24	1.50%		1.50%		50	-1.17%		-1.17%
25	-0.13%		-0.13%		51	0.85%		0.85%
26	0.23%		0.23%		52	3.01%		3.01%
27	1.56%		1.56%		53	-1.73%		-1.73%
					Averages	1.07%	-2.00%	0.72%

Figures from: 01/02/2009 to: 12/28/2017

HISTORICAL YEARLY RETURNS

| Year | Market Value | | Annual Returns | | Win |
	Buy & Hold Strategy	Trading Strategy	Buy & Hold Strategy	Trading Strategy	
2008	$ 10,000	$ 10,000	0%	0%	Y
2009	$ 15,043	$ 13,052	50%	31%	N
2010	$ 21,032	$ 23,014	40%	76%	Y
2011	$ 17,897	$ 38,346	-15%	67%	Y
2012	$ 25,783	$ 62,036	44%	62%	Y
2013	$ 56,302	$ 128,343	118%	107%	N
2014	$ 77,411	$ 173,817	37%	35%	N
2015	$ 73,139	$ 189,153	-6%	9%	Y
2016	$ 95,087	$ 248,372	30%	31%	Y
2017	$ 163,713	$ 452,234	72%	82%	Y
Averages	-	-	**37.2%**	**50.0%**	**70.0%**

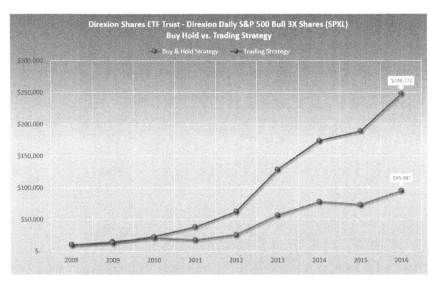

Direxion Shares ETF Trust - Direxion Daily S&P 500 Bull 3X Shares (SPXL)
Buy Hold vs. Trading Strategy

DIREXION DAILY S&P500® BEAR 3X SHARES (SPXS)

SUMMARY

Ticker: SPXS

Description: The investment seeks daily investment results, before fees and expenses, of 300% of the inverse (or opposite) of the performance of the S&P 500® Index. The fund, under normal circumstances, creates short positions by investing at least 80% of its assets in: futures contracts; options on securities, indices and futures contracts; equity caps, floors and collars; swap agreements; forward contracts; short positions; reverse repurchase agreements; exchange-traded funds ("ETFs"); and other financial instruments that, in combination, provide inverse leveraged and unleveraged exposure to the S&P 500® Index ("index"). The fund is non-diversified.

Data From: 1/2/2009 To: 12/28/2017		Total Return		
Winning Probability		• Buy & Hold:		-99.55%
• Monthly:	78.70%	• Trading Strategy:		-27.60%
• Annually:	100.00%	Trading Weeks:		
			BUY	SELL
Average Annual Returns			19	22
• Buy & Hold:	-38.98%		31	42
• Trading Strategy:	-1.71%			
• Delta:	37.27%			

⚠ NOTE: It is not advisable to be in short ETF's positions for a long period of time. Timing on Shorts are key to making a profit in a short amount of time. Frequently adjust your stop losses to ensure you lock in profits.

MONTHLY ANALYSIS

Month	Average Return Buy & Hold Strategy	Average Return Trading Strategy	Standard Dev of Month Return (Volatility)	Percentage Wins
Jan	5.09%	0.00%	12.88%	44.44%
Feb	-4.13%	0.00%	13.69%	88.89%
Mar	-9.52%	0.00%	12.97%	77.78%
Apr	-5.57%	0.00%	8.01%	77.78%
May	0.82%	2.77%	14.30%	77.78%
Jun	-0.38%	0.00%	8.49%	44.44%
Jul	-6.93%	1.95%	10.55%	100.00%
Aug	2.74%	2.74%	11.45%	100.00%
Sep	-4.62%	-4.62%	10.39%	100.00%
Oct	-10.08%	-4.70%	13.17%	66.67%
Nov	-7.03%	0.00%	5.91%	77.78%
Dec	-4.92%	0.00%	5.18%	88.89%
Averages	-3.71%	-0.15%	11.38%	78.70%

Figures from: 01/02/2009 to: 12/28/2017

WEEKLY AVERAGE RETURNS

Week No.	BUY	SELL	Buy & Hold
1		0.70%	0.70%
2		0.91%	0.91%
3		0.20%	0.20%
4		0.24%	0.24%
5		0.24%	0.24%
6		3.16%	3.16%
7		1.93%	1.93%
8		0.26%	0.26%
9		1.22%	1.22%
10		1.77%	1.77%
11		3.98%	3.98%
12		1.17%	1.17%
13		0.18%	0.18%
14		2.36%	2.36%
15		0.69%	0.69%
16		1.76%	1.76%
17		4.27%	4.27%
18		0.66%	0.66%
19	3.13%		3.13%
20	2.70%		2.70%
21	2.04%		2.04%
22		0.93%	0.93%
23		0.20%	0.20%
24		1.66%	1.66%
25		0.03%	0.03%
26		0.42%	0.42%
27		1.16%	1.16%

Week No.	BUY	SELL	Buy & Hold
27		-1.16%	-1.16%
28		-3.04%	-3.04%
29		-2.56%	-2.56%
30		-3.39%	-3.39%
31	0.93%		0.93%
32	2.97%		2.97%
33	0.02%		0.02%
34	2.73%		2.73%
35		-3.23%	-3.23%
36		-1.11%	-1.11%
37		-1.10%	-1.10%
38		-2.64%	-2.64%
39	3.14%		3.14%
40	-0.25%		-0.25%
41	-3.06%		-3.06%
42		-2.35%	-2.35%
43		-2.60%	-2.60%
44		-0.92%	-0.92%
45		-0.93%	-0.93%
46		0.73%	0.73%
47		-0.94%	-0.94%
48		0.54%	0.54%
49		-3.77%	-3.77%
50		1.17%	1.17%
51		-1.09%	-1.09%
52		-2.88%	-2.88%
53		1.66%	1.66%
Averages	0.45%	-1.24%	-0.79%

Figures from: 01/02/2009 to: 12/28/2017

114

HISTORICAL YEARLY RETURNS

	Market Value		Annual Returns		
Year	Buy & Hold Strategy	Trading Strategy	Buy & Hold Strategy	Trading Strategy	Win
2008	$ 10,000	$ 10,000	0%	0%	Y
2009	$ 3,211	$ 6,727	-68%	-33%	Y
2010	$ 1,646	$ 6,691	-49%	-1%	Y
2011	$ 1,108	$ 9,387	-33%	40%	Y
2012	$ 635	$ 9,223	-43%	-2%	Y
2013	$ 249	$ 8,082	-61%	-12%	Y
2014	$ 155	$ 8,386	-38%	4%	Y
2015	$ 127	$ 8,193	-18%	-2%	Y
2016	$ 81	$ 8,294	-36%	1%	Y
2017	$ 45	$ 7,240	-45%	-13%	Y
Averages	-	-	-39.0%	-1.7%	100.0%

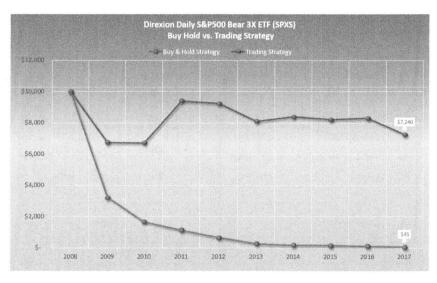

115

DAILY ENERGY BULL 3X SHARES (ERX)

SUMMARY

Ticker: ERX

Description: The investment seeks daily investment results, before fees and expenses, of 300% of the performance of the Energy Select Sector Index. The fund creates long positions by investing at least 80% of its assets in the securities that comprise the Energy Select Sector Index and/or financial instruments that provide leveraged and unleveraged exposure to the index. These financial instruments include: futures contracts; options on securities, indices and futures contracts; equity caps, floors and collars; swap agreements; forward contracts; short positions; reverse repurchase agreements; exchange-traded funds; and other financial instruments. It is non-diversified.

Data From: 1/2/2009 To: 12/28/2017		Total Return		
Winning Probability		• Buy & Hold:		-10.10%
• Monthly:	87.04%	• Trading Strategy:		553.18%
• Annually:	80.00%	Trading Weeks:		
			BUY	SELL
Average Annual Returns			6	1
• Buy & Hold:	8.27%		26	19
• Trading Strategy:	27.49%		49	46
• Delta:	19.22%			

MONTHLY ANALYSIS

Month	Average Return Buy & Hold Strategy	Average Return Trading Strategy	Standard Dev of Month Return (Volatility)	Percentage Wins
Jan	-7.52%	0.89%	15.84%	77.78%
Feb	1.24%	-0.03%	16.08%	77.78%
Mar	5.82%	5.82%	13.76%	100.00%
Apr	7.53%	7.53%	13.82%	100.00%
May	-7.18%	-0.77%	19.38%	66.67%
Jun	-1.44%	-0.94%	14.89%	55.56%
Jul	3.34%	3.34%	14.28%	100.00%
Aug	-7.37%	-7.37%	15.58%	100.00%
Sep	3.23%	3.23%	21.41%	100.00%
Oct	13.06%	13.06%	26.17%	100.00%
Nov	2.63%	9.07%	14.19%	66.67%
Dec	0.60%	0.60%	14.71%	100.00%
Averages	1.16%	2.87%	17.27%	87.04%

Figures from: 01/02/2009 to: 12/28/2017

WEEKLY AVERAGE RETURNS

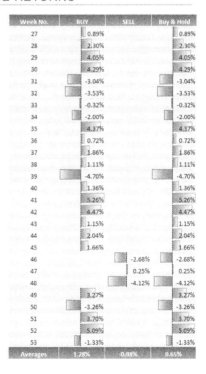

Week No.	BUY	SELL	Buy & Hold
1		-0.24%	-0.24%
2		-4.07%	-4.07%
3		2.18%	2.18%
4		0.92%	0.92%
5		1.88%	1.88%
6	2.92%		2.92%
7	0.54%		0.54%
8	-1.20%		-1.20%
9	-0.25%		-0.25%
10	2.50%		2.50%
11	0.71%		0.71%
12	0.64%		0.64%
13	-0.57%		-0.57%
14	2.25%		2.25%
15	0.44%		0.44%
16	1.99%		1.99%
17	7.01%		7.01%
18	1.59%		1.59%
19		-4.89%	-4.89%
20		-3.29%	-3.29%
21		-3.15%	-3.15%
22		0.73%	0.73%
23		1.13%	1.13%
24		3.41%	3.41%
25		-2.48%	-2.48%
26	0.30%		0.30%
27	0.89%		0.89%

Week No.	BUY	SELL	Buy & Hold
27	0.89%		0.89%
28	2.30%		2.30%
29	4.05%		4.05%
30	4.29%		4.29%
31	-3.04%		-3.04%
32	-3.53%		-3.53%
33	-0.32%		-0.32%
34	-2.00%		-2.00%
35	4.37%		4.37%
36	0.72%		0.72%
37	1.86%		1.86%
38	1.11%		1.11%
39	-4.70%		-4.70%
40	1.36%		1.36%
41	5.26%		5.26%
42	4.47%		4.47%
43	1.15%		1.15%
44	2.04%		2.04%
45	1.66%		1.66%
46		-2.68%	-2.68%
47		0.25%	0.25%
48		-4.12%	-4.12%
49	3.27%		3.27%
50	-3.26%		-3.26%
51	3.70%		3.70%
52	5.09%		5.09%
53	-1.33%		-1.33%
Averages	1.28%	-0.98%	0.65%

Figures from: 01/02/2009 to: 12/28/2017

117

HISTORICAL YEARLY RETURNS

Year	Market Value		Annual Returns		Win
	Buy & Hold Strategy	Trading Strategy	Buy & Hold Strategy	Trading Strategy	
2008	$ 10,000	$ 10,000	0%	0%	Y
2009	$ 9,981	$ 12,160	0%	22%	Y
2010	$ 14,862	$ 27,309	49%	125%	Y
2011	$ 11,912	$ 38,744	-20%	42%	Y
2012	$ 12,327	$ 41,622	3%	7%	Y
2013	$ 22,853	$ 62,666	85%	51%	N
2014	$ 15,375	$ 54,669	-33%	-13%	Y
2015	$ 5,957	$ 35,623	-61%	-35%	Y
2016	$ 10,148	$ 59,121	70%	66%	N
2017	$ 8,990	$ 65,318	-11%	10%	Y
Averages	-	-	8.3%	27.5%	80.0%

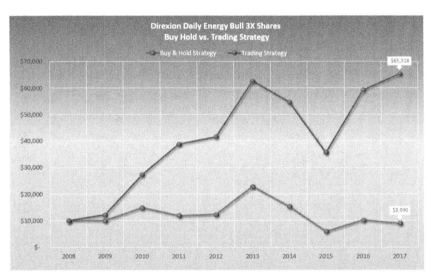

DAILY ENERGY BEAR 3X SHARES (ERY)

SUMMARY

Ticker: ERY

Description: The investment seeks daily investment results, before fees and expenses, of 300% of the inverse (or opposite) of the performance of the Energy Select Sector Index. The fund, under normal circumstances, creates short positions by investing at least 80% of its assets in: futures contracts; options on securities, indices and futures contracts; equity caps, floors and collars; swap agreements; forward contracts; short positions; reverse repurchase agreements; exchange-traded funds ("ETFs"); and other financial instruments that, in combination, provide inverse leveraged and unleveraged exposure to the Energy Select Sector Index. The fund is non-diversified.

Data From: 1/2/2009 To: 12/28/2017		Total Return		
Winning Probability		• Buy & Hold:		-99.09%
• Monthly:	69.44%	• Trading Strategy:		33.02%
• Annually:	90.00%	Trading Weeks:		
		BUY	SELL	
Average Annual Returns		19	6	
• Buy & Hold:	-29.31%	46	26	
• Trading Strategy:	5.06%	52	49	
• Delta:	34.36%			

⚠ NOTE: It is not advisable to be in short ETF's positions for a long period of time. Timing on Shorts are key to making a profit in a short amount of time. Frequently adjust your stop losses to ensure you lock in profits.

MONTHLY ANALYSIS

Month	Average Return Buy & Hold Strategy	Average Return Trading Strategy	Standard Dev of Month Return (Volatility)	Percentage Wins
Jan	4.60%	5.40%	14.08%	100.00%
Feb	-2.89%	-1.26%	14.84%	77.78%
Mar	-7.83%	0.00%	15.01%	66.67%
Apr	-8.52%	0.00%	11.93%	66.67%
May	7.63%	6.29%	22.77%	77.78%
Jun	-0.97%	-0.88%	14.48%	55.56%
Jul	-4.46%	0.00%	14.10%	66.67%
Aug	3.80%	0.00%	13.52%	44.44%
Sep	-2.62%	0.00%	21.35%	66.67%
Oct	-11.43%	0.00%	18.85%	55.56%
Nov	-4.87%	4.60%	13.84%	88.89%
Dec	-1.97%	-3.73%	15.11%	66.67%
Averages	-2.46%	0.87%	16.22%	69.44%

Figures from: 01/02/2009 to: 12/28/2017

WEEKLY AVERAGE RETURNS

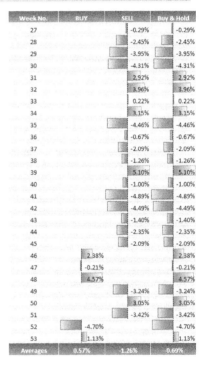

Week No.	BUY	SELL	Buy & Hold
1	0.18%		0.18%
2	3.99%		3.99%
3	-2.91%		-2.91%
4	-1.25%		-1.25%
5	-1.64%		-1.64%
6		-3.10%	-3.10%
7		-0.67%	-0.67%
8		1.10%	1.10%
9		-0.37%	-0.37%
10		-2.62%	-2.62%
11		-1.20%	-1.20%
12		-1.23%	-1.23%
13		0.60%	0.60%
14		-2.13%	-2.13%
15		-0.80%	-0.80%
16		-2.17%	-2.17%
17		-6.81%	-6.81%
18		-1.80%	-1.80%
19	5.57%		5.57%
20	3.14%		3.14%
21	2.96%		2.96%
22	-0.64%		-0.64%
23	-1.79%		-1.79%
24	-3.69%		-3.69%
25	2.45%		2.45%
26		-0.20%	-0.20%
27		-0.29%	-0.29%

Week No.	BUY	SELL	Buy & Hold
27		-0.29%	-0.29%
28		-2.45%	-2.45%
29		-3.95%	-3.95%
30		-4.31%	-4.31%
31		2.92%	2.92%
32		3.96%	3.96%
33		0.22%	0.22%
34		3.15%	3.15%
35		-4.46%	-4.46%
36		-0.67%	-0.67%
37		-2.09%	-2.09%
38		-1.26%	-1.26%
39		5.10%	5.10%
40		-1.00%	-1.00%
41		-4.89%	-4.89%
42		-4.49%	-4.49%
43		-1.40%	-1.40%
44		-2.35%	-2.35%
45		-2.09%	-2.09%
46	2.38%		2.38%
47	-0.21%		-0.21%
48	4.57%		4.57%
49		-3.24%	-3.24%
50		3.05%	3.05%
51		-3.42%	-3.42%
52	-4.70%		-4.70%
53	1.13%		1.13%
Averages	0.57%	-1.26%	-0.69%

Figures from: 01/02/2009 to: 12/28/2017

120

| Year | Market Value | | Annual Returns | | Win |
	Buy & Hold Strategy	Trading Strategy	Buy & Hold Strategy	Trading Strategy	
2008	$ 10,000	$ 10,000	0%	0%	Y
2009	$ 3,460	$ 8,295	-65%	-17%	Y
2010	$ 1,383	$ 9,001	-60%	9%	Y
2011	$ 694	$ 12,076	-50%	34%	Y
2012	$ 480	$ 11,609	-31%	-4%	Y
2013	$ 206	$ 8,314	-57%	-28%	Y
2014	$ 215	$ 10,392	4%	25%	Y
2015	$ 300	$ 13,961	40%	34%	N
2016	$ 97	$ 11,569	-67%	-17%	Y
2017	$ 91	$ 13,302	-6%	15%	Y
Averages	-	-	-29.3%	5.1%	90.0%

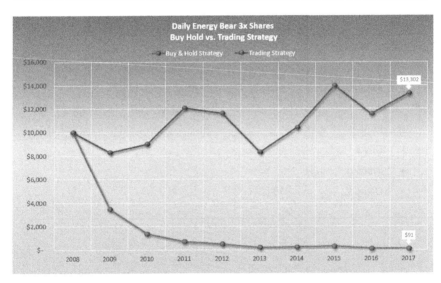

Daily Energy Bear 3x Shares
Buy Hold vs. Trading Strategy

DAILY TECHNOLOGY BULL 3X SHARES (TECL)

SUMMARY

Ticker: TECL

Description: The investment seeks daily investment results, before fees and expenses, of 300% of the performance of the Technology Select Sector Index. The fund creates long positions by investing at least 80% of its assets in the securities that comprise the Technology Select Sector Index and/or financial instruments that provide leveraged and unleveraged exposure to the index. These financial instruments include: futures contracts; options on securities, indices and futures contracts; equity caps, floors and collars; swap agreements; forward contracts; short positions; reverse repurchase agreements; exchange-traded funds ("ETFs"); etc. It is non-diversified.

Data From: 1/2/2009 To: 12/28/2017		Total Return		
Winning Probability		• Buy & Hold:	4,085.88%	
• Monthly:	85.19%	• Trading Strategy:	12,102.76%	
• Annually:	60.00%	Trading Weeks:		
		BUY	**SELL**	
Average Annual Returns		6	3	
• Buy & Hold:	58.50%			
• Trading Strategy:	78.33%	22	19	
• Delta:	19.83%	36	32	

MONTHLY ANALYSIS

Month	Average Return Buy & Hold Strategy	Average Return Trading Strategy	Standard Dev of Month Return (Volatility)	Percentage Wins
Jan	-4.69%	-1.24%	15.40%	55.56%
Feb	6.44%	5.67%	13.32%	77.78%
Mar	9.89%	9.89%	16.53%	100.00%
Apr	3.72%	3.72%	13.30%	100.00%
May	-0.36%	3.76%	14.66%	44.44%
Jun	-3.97%	-3.97%	9.82%	100.00%
Jul	11.52%	11.52%	10.23%	100.00%
Aug	-3.82%	0.57%	14.66%	44.44%
Sep	6.83%	6.83%	11.62%	100.00%
Oct	14.17%	14.17%	18.93%	100.00%
Nov	3.58%	3.58%	7.10%	100.00%
Dec	3.85%	3.85%	9.27%	100.00%
Averages	3.93%	4.86%	13.96%	85.19%

Figures from: 12/31/2008 to: 12/28/2017

WEEKLY AVERAGE RETURNS

Week No.	BUY	SELL	Buy & Hold
1	0.45%		0.45%
2	-1.24%		-1.24%
3		0.37%	0.37%
4		0.26%	0.26%
5		-0.78%	-0.78%
6	5.27%		5.27%
7	2.58%		2.58%
8	0.18%		0.18%
9	1.45%		1.45%
10	1.76%		1.76%
11	4.49%		4.49%
12	1.57%		1.57%
13	-0.10%		-0.10%
14	2.54%		2.54%
15	0.00%		0.00%
16	0.33%		0.33%
17	5.03%		5.03%
18	-0.51%		-0.51%
19		-4.76%	-4.76%
20		-1.97%	-1.97%
21		-2.34%	-2.34%
22	1.97%		1.97%
23	-0.63%		-0.63%
24	0.38%		0.38%
25	-0.03%		-0.03%
26	-0.38%		-0.38%
27	2.10%		2.10%

Week No.	BUY	SELL	Buy & Hold
27	2.10%		2.10%
28	3.39%		3.39%
29	4.38%		4.38%
30	3.25%		3.25%
31	-0.38%		-0.38%
32		-3.14%	-3.14%
33		-0.32%	-0.32%
34		-2.98%	-2.98%
35		3.94%	3.94%
36	0.68%		0.68%
37	0.85%		0.85%
38	4.04%		4.04%
39	-1.74%		-1.74%
40	-0.64%		-0.64%
41	3.26%		3.26%
42	2.82%		2.82%
43	2.66%		2.66%
44	1.00%		1.00%
45	0.45%		0.45%
46	-2.09%		-2.09%
47	1.28%		1.28%
48	-1.04%		-1.04%
49	2.88%		2.88%
50	-0.99%		-0.99%
51	0.48%		0.48%
52	2.27%		2.27%
53	-2.05%		-2.05%
Averages	1.22%	-1.17%	0.77%

Figures from: 12/31/2008 to: 12/28/2017

123

Year	Market Value		Annual Returns		Win
	Buy & Hold Strategy	Trading Strategy	Buy & Hold Strategy	Trading Strategy	
2008	$ 10,000	$ 10,000	0%	0%	Y
2009	$ 33,867	$ 40,751	239%	308%	Y
2010	$ 40,928	$ 108,695	21%	167%	Y
2011	$ 33,413	$ 135,630	-18%	25%	Y
2012	$ 44,669	$ 157,621	34%	16%	N
2013	$ 83,692	$ 302,355	87%	92%	Y
2014	$ 127,600	$ 402,796	52%	33%	N
2015	$ 133,577	$ 536,489	5%	33%	Y
2016	$ 183,114	$ 641,161	37%	20%	N
2017	$ 418,588	$ 1,220,276	129%	90%	N
Averages	-	-	58.5%	78.3%	60.0%

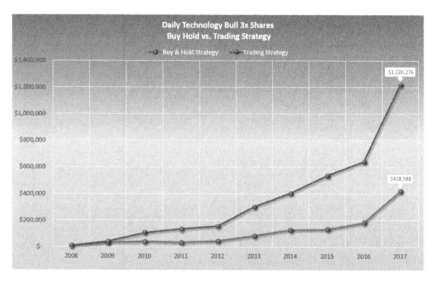

Daily Technology Bull 3x Shares
Buy Hold vs. Trading Strategy

DAILY TECHNOLOGY BEAR 3X SHARES (TECS)

SUMMARY

Ticker: TECS

Description: The investment seeks daily investment results, before fees and expenses, of 300% of the inverse (or opposite) of the performance of the Technology Select Sector Index. The fund, under normal circumstances, creates short positions by investing at least 80% of its assets in: futures contracts; options on securities, indices and futures contracts; equity caps, floors and collars; swap agreements; forward contracts; short positions; reverse repurchase agreements; exchange-traded funds ("ETFs"); and other financial instruments that, in combination, provide inverse leveraged and unleveraged exposure to the Technology Select Sector Index. It is non-diversified.

Data From: 01/2/2009 To: 12/28/2017		Total Return		
Winning Probability		• Buy & Hold:		-99.89%
• Monthly:	69.44%	• Trading Strategy:		28.39%
• Annually:	100.00%	Trading Weeks:		
		BUY	**SELL**	
Average Annual Returns		4	6	
• Buy & Hold:	-44.34%	19	22	
• Trading Strategy:	5.94%			
• Delta:	50.28%	32	36	

⚠ NOTE: Over the past 5 years this strategy has had a very low annual return, recommended not to use this strategy at this time.

⚠ NOTE: It is not advisable to be in short ETF's positions for a long period of time. Timing on Shorts are key to making a profit in a short amount of time. Frequently adjust your stop losses to ensure you lock in profits.

MONTHLY ANALYSIS

Month	Average Return Buy & Hold Strategy	Average Return Trading Strategy	Standard Dev of Month Return (Volatility)	Percentage Wins
Jan	3.46%	1.87%	14.98%	44.44%
Feb	-7.21%	-0.71%	9.97%	66.67%
Mar	-9.96%	0.00%	15.06%	77.78%
Apr	-4.44%	0.00%	13.03%	66.67%
May	-0.34%	3.57%	15.06%	77.78%
Jun	2.25%	0.00%	9.95%	33.33%
Jul	11.64%	0.00%	8.43%	100.00%
Aug	1.83%	2.42%	13.78%	66.67%
Sep	-7.58%	0.00%	8.87%	77.78%
Oct	-12.15%	0.00%	16.07%	77.78%
Nov	-5.37%	0.00%	5.96%	77.78%
Dec	-4.74%	0.00%	7.77%	66.67%
Averages	-4.66%	0.60%	12.54%	69.44%

Figures from: 12/31/2008 to: 12/28/2017

WEEKLY AVERAGE RETURNS

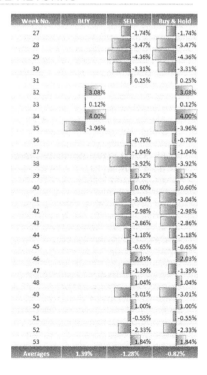

Week No.	BUY	SELL	Buy & Hold
1		-0.41%	-0.41%
2		0.92%	0.92%
3		-0.90%	-0.90%
4	-0.29%		-0.29%
5	0.39%		0.39%
6		-4.76%	-4.76%
7		-2.74%	-2.74%
8		-0.29%	-0.29%
9		-1.86%	-1.86%
10		-1.95%	-1.95%
11		-3.74%	-3.74%
12		-1.72%	-1.72%
13		-0.27%	-0.27%
14		-2.11%	-2.11%
15		-0.37%	-0.37%
16		-0.70%	-0.70%
17		-4.73%	-4.73%
18		0.51%	0.51%
19	5.16%		5.16%
20	1.70%		1.70%
21	2.34%		2.34%
22		-2.09%	-2.09%
23		0.47%	0.47%
24		-0.56%	-0.56%
25		-0.12%	-0.12%
26		0.10%	0.10%
27		-1.74%	-1.74%

Week No.	BUY	SELL	Buy & Hold
27		-1.74%	-1.74%
28		-3.47%	-3.47%
29		-4.36%	-4.36%
30		-3.31%	-3.31%
31		0.25%	0.25%
32	3.08%		3.08%
33	0.12%		0.12%
34	4.00%		4.00%
35	-3.96%		-3.96%
36		-0.70%	-0.70%
37		-1.04%	-1.04%
38		-3.92%	-3.92%
39		1.52%	1.52%
40		0.60%	0.60%
41		-3.04%	-3.04%
42		-2.98%	-2.98%
43		-2.86%	-2.86%
44		-1.18%	-1.18%
45		-0.65%	-0.65%
46		2.03%	2.03%
47		-1.39%	-1.39%
48		1.04%	1.04%
49		-3.01%	-3.01%
50		1.00%	1.00%
51		-0.55%	-0.55%
52		-2.33%	-2.33%
53		1.84%	1.84%
Averages	1.39%	-1.28%	-0.82%

Figures from: 12/31/2008 to: 12/28/2017

Year	Market Value		Annual Returns		Win
	Buy & Hold Strategy	Trading Strategy	Buy & Hold Strategy	Trading Strategy	
2008	$ 10,000	$ 10,000	0%	0%	Y
2009	$ 1,353	$ 9,284	-86%	-7%	Y
2010	$ 740	$ 17,116	-45%	84%	Y
2011	$ 505	$ 22,966	-32%	34%	Y
2012	$ 290	$ 21,283	-43%	-7%	Y
2013	$ 130	$ 20,871	-55%	-2%	Y
2014	$ 70	$ 18,560	-46%	-11%	Y
2015	$ 48	$ 20,212	-31%	9%	Y
2016	$ 27	$ 15,814	-43%	-22%	Y
2017	$ 11	$ 12,839	-61%	-19%	Y
Averages	-	-	-44.3%	5.9%	100.0%

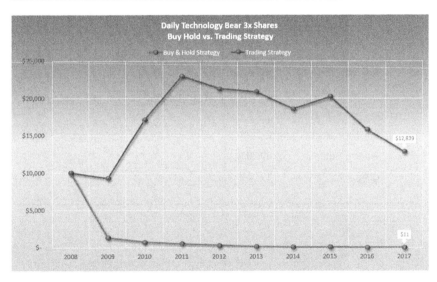

DIREXION DAILY FINANCIAL BULL 3X SHARES (FAS)

SUMMARY

Ticker: FAS

Description: The investment seeks daily investment results, before fees and expenses, of 300% of the performance of the Russell 1000® Financial Services Index. The fund creates long positions by investing at least 80% of its assets in the securities that comprise the Russell 1000® Financial Services Index and/or financial instruments that provide leveraged and unleveraged exposure to the index. These financial instruments include: futures contracts; options on securities, indices and futures contracts; equity caps, floors and collars; swap agreements; forward contracts; short positions; reverse repurchase agreements; exchange-traded funds; etc. It is non-diversified.

Data From: 1/2/2009 To: 12/28/2017		Total Return		
Winning Probability		• Buy & Hold:		295.00%
• Monthly:	92.66%	• Trading Strategy:		1,018.47%
• Annually:	70.00%	Trading Weeks:		
			BUY	SELL
Average Annual Returns			36	33
• Buy & Hold:	27.12%			
• Trading Strategy:	39.50%		23	20
• Delta:	12.37%			

MONTHLY ANALYSIS

Month	Average Return Buy & Hold Strategy	Average Return Trading Strategy	Standard Dev of Month Return (Volatility)	Percentage Wins
Jan	-10.64%	-10.64%	23.26%	100.00%
Feb	0.94%	0.94%	19.58%	100.00%
Mar	10.72%	10.72%	15.78%	100.00%
Apr	4.19%	4.19%	13.20%	100.00%
May	-1.38%	3.48%	18.89%	66.67%
Jun	-0.27%	-0.23%	13.10%	100.00%
Jul	6.41%	6.41%	13.02%	100.00%
Aug	-4.32%	0.13%	20.49%	44.44%
Sep	1.83%	1.83%	13.52%	100.00%
Oct	11.63%	11.63%	18.58%	100.00%
Nov	5.87%	5.87%	10.63%	100.00%
Dec	5.66%	5.66%	9.04%	100.00%
Averages	2.55%	3.33%	16.53%	92.66%

Figures from: 12/31/2008 to: 12/28/2017

WEEKLY AVERAGE RETURNS

Week No.	BUY	SELL	Buy & Hold
1	1.29%		1.29%
2	-1.55%		-1.55%
3	-2.40%		-2.40%
4	-0.16%		-0.16%
5	2.92%		2.92%
6	2.89%		2.89%
7	-0.11%		-0.11%
8	-1.97%		-1.97%
9	2.57%		2.57%
10	-0.14%		-0.14%
11	12.27%		12.27%
12	0.91%		0.91%
13	-2.15%		-2.15%
14	5.33%		5.33%
15	1.83%		1.83%
16	0.02%		0.02%
17	6.42%		6.42%
18	-0.04%		-0.04%
19	-0.89%		-0.89%
20		-5.26%	-5.26%
21		-2.59%	-2.59%
22		0.65%	0.65%
23	1.13%		1.13%
24	1.44%		1.44%
25	-0.54%		-0.54%
26	2.23%		2.23%
27	1.02%		1.02%

Week No.	BUY	SELL	Buy & Hold
27	1.02%		1.02%
28	2.80%		2.80%
29	0.68%		0.68%
30	3.68%		3.68%
31	0.14%		0.14%
32	-1.40%		-1.40%
33		-1.19%	-1.19%
34		-1.55%	-1.55%
35		3.43%	3.43%
36	0.42%		0.42%
37	1.92%		1.92%
38	1.81%		1.81%
39	-3.90%		-3.90%
40	-0.35%		-0.35%
41	2.82%		2.82%
42	1.05%		1.05%
43	3.51%		3.51%
44	0.71%		0.71%
45	0.78%		0.78%
46	-1.06%		-1.06%
47	0.04%		0.04%
48	-1.04%		-1.04%
49	5.08%		5.08%
50	-0.64%		-0.64%
51	0.51%		0.51%
52	4.13%		4.13%
53	-1.38%		-1.38%
Averages	1.12%	-1.09%	0.87%

Figures from: 12/31/2008 to: 12/28/2017

129

Year	Market Value		Annual Returns		Win
	Buy & Hold Strategy	Trading Strategy	Buy & Hold Strategy	Trading Strategy	
2008	$ 10,000	$ 10,000	0%	0%	Y
2009	$ 5,854	$ 6,970	-41%	-30%	Y
2010	$ 6,616	$ 10,876	13%	56%	Y
2011	$ 3,083	$ 6,753	-53%	-38%	Y
2012	$ 5,699	$ 15,789	85%	134%	Y
2013	$ 12,875	$ 39,301	126%	149%	Y
2014	$ 18,129	$ 47,220	41%	20%	N
2015	$ 16,579	$ 53,284	-9%	13%	Y
2016	$ 23,326	$ 69,384	41%	30%	N
2017	$ 39,500	$ 111,847	69%	61%	N
Averages	-	-	27.1%	39.5%	70.0%

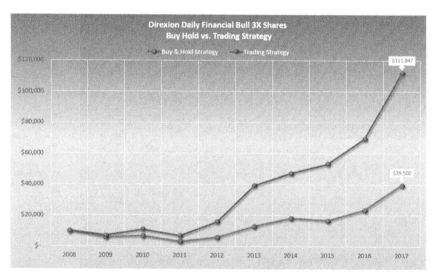

DIREXION DAILY FINANCIAL BEAR 3X SHARES (FAZ)

SUMMARY

Ticker: FAZ

Description: The investment seeks daily investment results, before fees and expenses, of 300% of the inverse (or opposite) of the performance of the Russell 1000® Financial Services Index. The fund creates short positions by investing at least 80% of its assets in: futures contracts; options on securities, indices and futures contracts; equity caps, floors and collars; swap agreements; forward contracts; short positions; reverse repurchase agreements; exchange-traded funds; and other financial instruments that, in combination, provide inverse leveraged and unleveraged exposure to the Russell 1000® Financial Services Index. It is non-diversified.

Data From: 1/2/2009 To: 12/28/2017		Total Return		
Winning Probability		• Buy & Hold:		-99.96%
• Monthly:	66.67%	• Trading Strategy:		22.55%
• Annually:	100.00%	Trading Weeks:		
		BUY	SELL	
Average Annual Returns		33	36	
• Buy & Hold:	-44.47%			
• Trading Strategy:	2.78%	20	23	
• Delta:	47.25%			

⚠ NOTE: It is not advisable to be in short ETF's positions for a long period of time. Timing on Shorts are key to making a profit in a short amount of time. Frequently adjust your stop losses to ensure you lock in profits.

⚠ NOTE: The last 4 years the annual return has been very low, it is not recommended to use this strategy at this time.

MONTHLY ANALYSIS

Month	Average Return Buy & Hold Strategy	Average Return Trading Strategy	Standard Dev of Month Return (Volatility)	Percentage Wins
Jan	7.84%	0.00%	18.38%	33.33%
Feb	-4.55%	0.00%	12.25%	77.78%
Mar	-14.53%	0.00%	24.03%	77.78%
Apr	-8.11%	0.00%	19.14%	77.78%
May	-0.81%	0.65%	22.99%	33.33%
Jun	-2.24%	0.02%	10.21%	44.44%
Jul	-7.22%	0.00%	13.07%	77.78%
Aug	1.92%	1.71%	18.45%	44.44%
Sep	-3.76%	0.00%	11.97%	66.67%
Oct	-11.96%	0.00%	14.24%	100.00%
Nov	-7.80%	0.00%	7.96%	88.89%
Dec	-6.71%	0.00%	7.87%	77.78%
Averages	-4.83%	0.20%	16.12%	66.67%

Figures from: 12/31/2008 to: 12/28/2017

WEEKLY AVERAGE RETURNS

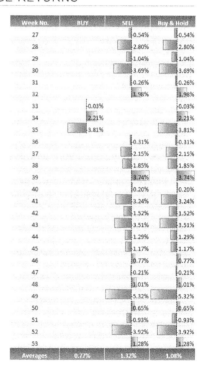

Week No.	BUY	SELL	Buy & Hold
1		1.41%	1.41%
2		1.42%	1.42%
3		2.71%	2.71%
4		1.37%	1.37%
5		4.52%	4.52%
6		3.15%	3.15%
7		0.63%	0.63%
8		1.83%	1.83%
9		4.07%	4.07%
10		0.95%	0.95%
11		9.03%	9.03%
12		2.83%	2.83%
13		1.41%	1.41%
14		4.13%	4.13%
15		2.88%	2.88%
16		1.14%	1.14%
17		6.42%	6.42%
18		0.51%	0.51%
19		1.01%	1.01%
20	5.10%		5.10%
21	2.29%		2.29%
22	1.13%		1.13%
23		1.48%	1.48%
24		1.47%	1.47%
25		0.17%	0.17%
26		2.26%	2.26%
27		0.54%	0.54%

Week No.	BUY	SELL	Buy & Hold
27		0.54%	0.54%
28		2.80%	2.80%
29		1.04%	1.04%
30		3.69%	3.69%
31		0.26%	0.26%
32		1.98%	1.98%
33	0.03%		0.03%
34	2.21%		2.21%
35	3.81%		3.81%
36		0.31%	0.31%
37		2.15%	2.15%
38		1.85%	1.85%
39		3.74%	3.74%
40		0.20%	0.20%
41		3.24%	3.24%
42		1.52%	1.52%
43		3.51%	3.51%
44		1.29%	1.29%
45		1.17%	1.17%
46		0.77%	0.77%
47		0.21%	0.21%
48		1.01%	1.01%
49		5.32%	5.32%
50		0.65%	0.65%
51		0.93%	0.93%
52		3.92%	3.92%
53		1.28%	1.28%
Averages	0.77%	1.32%	1.08%

HISTORICAL YEARLY RETURNS

| Year | Market Value | | Annual Returns | | Win |
	Buy & Hold Strategy	Trading Strategy	Buy & Hold Strategy	Trading Strategy	
2008	$ 10,000	$ 10,000	0%	0%	Y
2009	$ 544	$ 9,470	-95%	-5%	Y
2010	$ 265	$ 11,444	-51%	21%	Y
2011	$ 209	$ 11,398	-21%	0%	Y
2012	$ 85	$ 13,817	-60%	21%	Y
2013	$ 30	$ 14,824	-64%	7%	Y
2014	$ 18	$ 12,483	-41%	-15%	Y
2015	$ 14	$ 14,443	-19%	16%	Y
2016	$ 8	$ 13,096	-47%	-9%	Y
2017	$ 4	$ 12,255	-47%	6%	Y
Averages	-	-	-44.5%	2.8%	100.0%

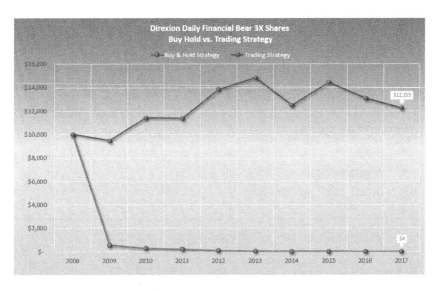

DAILY REAL ESTATE BULL 3X SHARES (DRN)

SUMMARY

Ticker: DRN

Description: The investment seeks daily investment results, before fees and expenses, of 300% of the performance of the MSCI US REIT IndexSM. The fund creates long positions by investing at least 80% of its assets in the securities that comprise the MSCI US REIT IndexSM and/or financial instruments that provide leveraged and unleveraged exposure to the index. These financial instruments include: futures contracts; options on securities, indices and futures contracts; equity caps, floors and collars; swap agreements; forward contracts; short positions; reverse repurchase agreements; exchange-traded funds; and other financial instruments. It is non-diversified.

Data From: 7/16/2009 To: 12/28/2017		Total Return	
Winning Probability		• Buy & Hold:	1,280.16%
• Monthly:	84.31%	• Trading Strategy:	9,721.09%
• Annually:	70.00%	Trading Weeks:	
		BUY	SELL
Average Annual Returns		24	19
• Buy & Hold:	38.14%		
• Trading Strategy:	74.63%	41	39
• Delta:	36.49%	49	44

MONTHLY ANALYSIS

Month	Average Return Buy & Hold Strategy	Average Return Trading Strategy	Standard Dev of Month Return (Volatility)	Percentage Wins
Jan	4.03%	4.03%	11.64%	100.00%
Feb	4.98%	4.98%	11.34%	100.00%
Mar	9.22%	9.22%	12.32%	100.00%
Apr	5.61%	5.61%	13.11%	100.00%
May	-7.20%	-0.57%	11.50%	62.50%
Jun	1.60%	1.45%	15.22%	50.00%
Jul	9.21%	9.21%	12.15%	100.00%
Aug	-4.83%	-4.83%	17.99%	100.00%
Sep	0.57%	7.82%	19.47%	77.78%
Oct	12.60%	13.11%	23.83%	55.56%
Nov	-1.53%	3.30%	10.01%	66.67%
Dec	9.53%	9.53%	7.06%	100.00%
Averages	3.65%	5.24%	15.01%	84.31%

Figures from: 07/16/2009 to: 12/28/2017

WEEKLY AVERAGE RETURNS

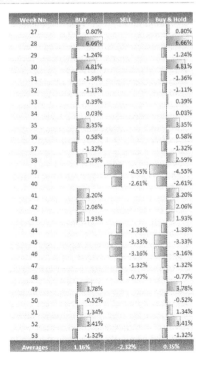

Week No.	BUY	SELL	Buy & Hold
1	1.09%		1.09%
2	0.24%		0.24%
3	1.11%		1.11%
4	-1.75%		-1.75%
5	1.78%		1.78%
6	-1.30%		-1.30%
7	1.23%		1.23%
8	2.11%		2.11%
9	-0.03%		-0.03%
10	-2.07%		-2.07%
11	4.42%		4.42%
12	2.61%		2.61%
13	0.38%		0.38%
14	2.17%		2.17%
15	-1.48%		-1.48%
16	1.45%		1.45%
17	3.73%		3.73%
18	-1.10%		-1.10%
19		-2.60%	-2.60%
20		-2.49%	-2.49%
21		-5.15%	-5.15%
22		0.84%	0.84%
23		-1.26%	-1.26%
24	3.42%		3.42%
25	0.45%		0.45%
26	0.70%		0.70%
27	0.80%		0.80%

Week No.	BUY	SELL	Buy & Hold
27	0.80%		0.80%
28	6.66%		6.66%
29	-1.24%		-1.24%
30	4.81%		4.81%
31	-1.36%		-1.36%
32	-1.11%		-1.11%
33	0.39%		0.39%
34	0.03%		0.03%
35	3.35%		3.35%
36	0.58%		0.58%
37	-1.32%		-1.32%
38	2.59%		2.59%
39		-4.55%	-4.55%
40		-2.61%	-2.61%
41	3.20%		3.20%
42	2.06%		2.06%
43	1.93%		1.93%
44		-1.38%	-1.38%
45		-3.33%	-3.33%
46		-3.16%	-3.16%
47		-1.32%	-1.32%
48		-0.77%	-0.77%
49	3.78%		3.78%
50	-0.52%		-0.52%
51	1.34%		1.34%
52	3.41%		3.41%
53	-1.32%		-1.32%
Averages	1.16%	-2.32%	0.35%

Figures from: 07/16/2009 to: 12/28/2017

135

Year	Market Value		Annual Returns		Win
	Buy & Hold Strategy	Trading Strategy	Buy & Hold Strategy	Trading Strategy	
2008	$ 10,000	$ 10,000	0%	0%	Y
2009	$ 25,098	$ 36,623	151%	266%	Y
2010	$ 40,945	$ 105,715	63%	189%	Y
2011	$ 38,861	$ 183,714	-5%	74%	Y
2012	$ 58,411	$ 310,422	50%	69%	Y
2013	$ 57,100	$ 516,186	-2%	66%	Y
2014	$ 118,887	$ 873,869	108%	69%	N
2015	$ 113,883	$ 944,616	-4%	8%	Y
2016	$ 129,213	$ 1,064,133	13%	13%	N
2017	$ 138,016	$ 982,109	7%	-8%	N
Averages	-	-	38.1%	74.6%	70.0%

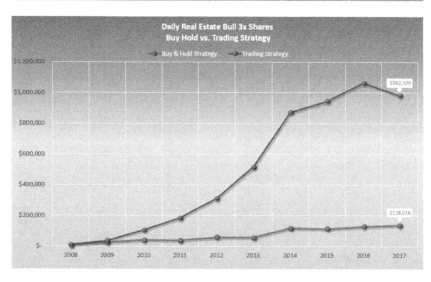

DAILY REAL ESTATE BEAR 3X SHARES (DRV)

SUMMARY

Ticker: DRV

Description: The investment seeks daily investment results, before fees and expenses, of 300% of the inverse (or opposite) of the performance of the MSCI US REIT IndexSM. The fund, under normal circumstances, creates short positions by investing at least 80% of its assets in: futures contracts; options on securities, indices and futures contracts; equity caps, floors and collars; swap agreements; forward contracts; short positions; reverse repurchase agreements; exchange-traded funds ("ETFs"); and other financial instruments that, in combination, provide inverse leveraged and unleveraged exposure to the MSCI US REIT IndexSM ("index"). The fund is non-diversified.

Data From: 7/16/2009 To: 12/28/2017		Total Return		
Winning Probability		• Buy & Hold:		-99.82%
• Monthly:	70.59%	• Trading Strategy:		160.63%
• Annually:	100.00%	Trading Weeks:		
			BUY	SELL
Average Annual Returns			19	24
• Buy & Hold:	-41.29%		39	41
• Trading Strategy:	12.91%		44	49
• Delta:	54.19%			

⚠ NOTE: It is not advisable to be in short ETF's positions for a long period of time. Timing on Shorts are key to making a profit in a short amount of time. Frequently adjust your stop losses to ensure you lock in profits.

MONTHLY ANALYSIS

Month	Average Return Buy & Hold Strategy	Average Return Trading Strategy	Standard Dev of Month Return (Volatility)	Percentage Wins
Jan	-4.85%	0.00%	10.37%	62.50%
Feb	-5.84%	0.00%	10.02%	75.00%
Mar	-9.41%	0.00%	9.93%	87.50%
Apr	-6.34%	0.00%	13.68%	75.00%
May	4.84%	4.33%	9.91%	75.00%
Jun	-3.10%	0.15%	13.04%	62.50%
Jul	-9.90%	0.00%	11.19%	77.78%
Aug	1.22%	0.00%	17.67%	44.44%
Sep	-1.53%	5.50%	18.79%	55.56%
Oct	-11.36%	0.51%	17.34%	66.67%
Nov	-1.09%	2.28%	11.01%	77.78%
Dec	-9.96%	0.00%	7.20%	88.89%
Averages	-4.78%	1.06%	13.28%	70.59%

Figures from: 07/16/2009 to: 12/28/2017

WEEKLY AVERAGE RETURNS

Week No.	BUY	SELL	Buy & Hold
1		-1.21%	-1.21%
2		-0.42%	-0.42%
3		-1.20%	-1.20%
4		1.80%	1.80%
5		-1.85%	-1.85%
6		0.99%	0.99%
7		-1.40%	-1.40%
8		-2.28%	-2.28%
9		-0.15%	-0.15%
10		2.28%	2.28%
11		-4.64%	-4.64%
12		-2.81%	-2.81%
13		-0.44%	-0.44%
14		-2.17%	-2.17%
15		1.25%	1.25%
16		-1.59%	-1.59%
17		-3.33%	-3.33%
18		0.38%	0.38%
19	3.02%		3.02%
20	2.49%		2.49%
21	4.95%		4.95%
22	-0.72%		-0.72%
23	1.30%		1.30%
24		-3.33%	-3.33%
25		-0.79%	-0.79%
26		-0.71%	-0.71%
27		-0.20%	-0.20%

Week No.	BUY	SELL	Buy & Hold
27		0.20%	0.20%
28		6.63%	6.63%
29		1.01%	1.01%
30		4.61%	4.61%
31		1.12%	1.12%
32		3.32%	3.32%
33		0.06%	0.06%
34		0.14%	0.14%
35		3.74%	3.74%
36		-0.81%	0.81%
37		1.10%	1.10%
38		2.47%	2.47%
39	4.09%		4.09%
40	3.75%		2.75%
41		3.58%	3.58%
42		2.70%	2.70%
43		2.08%	2.08%
44	0.87%		0.87%
45	3.17%		3.17%
46	2.76%		2.76%
47	0.99%		0.99%
48	0.65%		0.65%
49		4.02%	4.02%
50		0.31%	0.31%
51		1.57%	1.57%
52		3.33%	3.33%
53		1.13%	1.13%
Averages	2.19%	-1.20%	-0.42%

Figures from: 07/16/2009 to: 12/28/2017

138

HISTORICAL YEARLY RETURNS

Year	Market Value Buy & Hold Strategy	Market Value Trading Strategy	Annual Returns Buy & Hold Strategy	Annual Returns Trading Strategy	Win
2008	$ 10,000	$ 10,000	0%	0%	Y
2009	$ 2,174	$ 11,847	-78%	18%	Y
2010	$ 614	$ 15,770	-72%	33%	Y
2011	$ 265	$ 23,886	-57%	51%	Y
2012	$ 141	$ 25,088	-47%	5%	Y
2013	$ 110	$ 40,084	-22%	60%	Y
2014	$ 44	$ 31,576	-60%	-21%	Y
2015	$ 33	$ 33,150	-25%	5%	Y
2016	$ 22	$ 30,597	-35%	-8%	Y
2017	$ 18	$ 26,063	-17%	-15%	Y
Averages	-	-	-41.3%	12.9%	100.0%

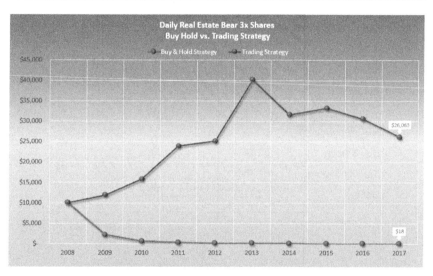

Daily Real Estate Bear 3x Shares
Buy Hold vs. Trading Strategy

DAILY RETAIL BULL 3X SHARES (RETL)

SUMMARY

Ticker: RETL

Description: The investment seeks daily investment results, before fees and expenses, of 300% of the performance of the Russell 1000® Retail Index. The fund creates long positions by investing at least 80% of its assets in the securities that comprise the Russell 1000® Retail Index and/or financial instruments that provide leveraged and unleveraged exposure to the index. These financial instruments include: futures contracts; options on securities, indices and futures contracts; equity caps, floors and collars; swap agreements; forward contracts; short positions; reverse repurchase agreements; exchange-traded funds; and other financial instruments. It is non-diversified.

Data From: 7/14/2010 To: 12/28/2017		Total Return		
Winning Probability		• Buy & Hold:	1,193.34%	
• Monthly:	87.78%	• Trading Strategy:	2,511.07%	
• Annually:	88.89%	Trading Weeks:		
		BUY	**SELL**	
Average Annual Returns		1	20	
• Buy & Hold:	38.74%			
• Trading Strategy:	51.46%	23	31	
• Delta:	12.71%	35	50	

MONTHLY ANALYSIS

Month	Average Return Buy & Hold Strategy	Average Return Trading Strategy	Standard Dev of Month Return (Volatility)	Percentage Wins
Jan	-2.30%	-2.30%	13.07%	100.00%
Feb	7.65%	7.65%	11.44%	100.00%
Mar	4.76%	4.76%	9.25%	100.00%
Apr	2.37%	2.37%	7.92%	100.00%
May	-2.58%	-0.28%	8.34%	71.43%
Jun	1.37%	1.61%	6.41%	100.00%
Jul	5.15%	5.99%	9.84%	62.50%
Aug	-2.73%	1.16%	15.30%	75.00%
Sep	6.33%	6.33%	9.55%	100.00%
Oct	4.22%	4.22%	12.83%	100.00%
Nov	13.46%	13.46%	11.05%	100.00%
Dec	0.47%	1.30%	8.79%	50.00%
Averages	3.18%	3.86%	11.01%	87.78%

Figures from: 07/14/2010 to: 12/28/2017

WEEKLY AVERAGE RETURNS

Week No.	BUY	SELL	Buy & Hold
1	-0.12%		-0.12%
2	-1.24%		-1.24%
3	-2.39%		-2.39%
4	2.95%		2.95%
5	0.49%		0.49%
6	2.79%		2.79%
7	3.32%		3.32%
8	-0.73%		-0.73%
9	2.43%		2.43%
10	1.55%		1.55%
11	1.70%		1.70%
12	-0.12%		-0.12%
13	0.97%		0.97%
14	0.84%		0.84%
15	-0.67%		-0.67%
16	2.70%		2.70%
17	2.87%		2.87%
18	0.63%		0.63%
19	-1.26%		-1.26%
20		-3.27%	-3.27%
21		-0.18%	-0.18%
22		-0.09%	-0.09%
23	1.91%		1.91%
24	-1.54%		-1.54%
25	-1.60%		-1.60%
26	2.87%		2.87%
27	3.28%		3.28%

Week No.	BUY	SELL	Buy & Hold
27	3.28%		3.28%
28	4.42%		4.42%
29	-0.57%		-0.57%
30	3.96%		3.96%
31		-0.24%	-0.24%
32		-3.18%	-3.18%
33		-1.54%	-1.54%
34		0.25%	0.25%
35	2.99%		2.99%
36	1.97%		1.97%
37	0.92%		0.92%
38	3.71%		3.71%
39	0.35%		0.35%
40	2.94%		2.94%
41	-0.83%		-0.83%
42	0.25%		0.25%
43	2.32%		2.32%
44	-0.15%		-0.15%
45	0.01%		0.01%
46	1.92%		1.92%
47	3.24%		3.24%
48	4.06%		4.06%
49	1.35%		1.35%
50		-1.00%	-1.00%
51		-1.23%	-1.23%
52		-0.68%	-0.68%
53		-1.31%	-1.31%
Averages	1.33%	-1.13%	0.80%

Figures from: 07/14/2010 to: 12/28/2017

141

HISTORICAL YEARLY RETURNS

Year	Market Value		Annual Returns		Win
	Buy & Hold Strategy	Trading Strategy	Buy & Hold Strategy	Trading Strategy	
2009	$ 10,000	$ 10,000	0%	0%	Y
2010	$ 14,909	$ 15,367	49%	54%	Y
2011	$ 15,961	$ 22,824	7%	49%	Y
2012	$ 28,366	$ 45,896	78%	101%	Y
2013	$ 67,404	$ 118,615	138%	158%	Y
2014	$ 89,463	$ 116,746	33%	-2%	N
2015	$ 129,080	$ 207,842	44%	78%	Y
2016	$ 128,072	$ 214,630	-1%	3%	Y
2017	$ 129,334	$ 261,107	1%	22%	Y
Averages	-	-	38.7%	51.5%	88.9%

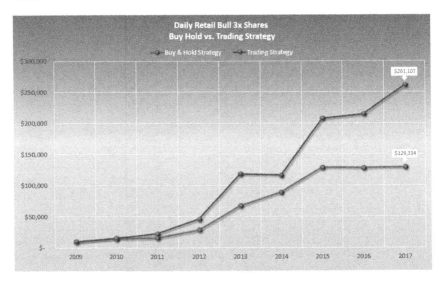

DIREXION DAILY GOLD MINERS BULL 3X ETF (NUGT)

SUMMARY

Ticker: NUGT

Description: The investment seeks daily investment results, before fees and expenses, of 300% of the performance of the NYSE Arca Gold Miners Index. The fund creates long positions by investing at least 80% of its assets in the securities that comprise the NYSE Arca Gold Miners Index and/or financial instruments that provide leveraged and unleveraged exposure to the index. These financial instruments include: futures contracts; options on securities, indices and futures contracts; equity caps, floors and collars; swap agreements; forward contracts; short positions; reverse repurchase agreements; exchange-traded funds; etc. It is non-diversified.

Data From: 1/3/3011 To: 12/28/2017		Total Return	
Winning Probability		• Buy & Hold:	-99.79%
• Monthly:	70.24%	• Trading Strategy:	1,013.19%
• Annually:	87.50%	Trading Weeks:	
		BUY	**SELL**
Average Annual Returns		33	6
• Buy & Hold:	-32.93%	52	35
• Trading Strategy:	42.18%		
• Delta:	75.10%		

MONTHLY ANALYSIS

Month	Average Return Buy & Hold Strategy	Average Return Trading Strategy	Standard Dev of Month Return (Volatility)	Percentage Wins
Jan	8.18%	8.35%	29.65%	100.00%
Feb	12.16%	1.04%	47.18%	57.14%
Mar	-12.64%	0.00%	19.57%	71.43%
Apr	4.77%	0.00%	47.21%	42.86%
May	-12.30%	0.00%	14.43%	85.71%
Jun	3.38%	0.00%	45.62%	71.43%
Jul	-2.21%	0.00%	25.90%	42.86%
Aug	8.87%	16.61%	27.68%	57.14%
Sep	-13.97%	0.00%	27.56%	85.71%
Oct	-6.22%	0.00%	26.27%	57.14%
Nov	-18.09%	0.00%	18.04%	85.71%
Dec	-8.80%	7.08%	17.46%	85.71%
Averages	-3.07%	2.76%	30.52%	70.24%

Figures from: 12/31/2010 to: 12/28/2017

WEEKLY AVERAGE RETURNS

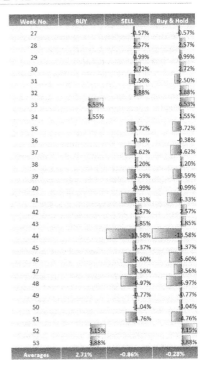

Week No.	BUY	SELL	Buy & Hold
1	-1.65%		-1.65%
2	3.62%		3.62%
3	-2.56%		-2.56%
4	-2.58%		-2.58%
5	7.35%		7.35%
6		6.12%	6.12%
7		2.95%	2.95%
8		1.78%	1.78%
9		-3.16%	-3.16%
10		-2.47%	-2.47%
11		0.51%	0.51%
12		4.31%	4.31%
13		-6.20%	-6.20%
14		-1.13%	-1.13%
15		5.11%	5.11%
16		-4.87%	-4.87%
17		2.56%	2.56%
18		6.06%	6.06%
19		-3.59%	-3.59%
20		-1.90%	-1.90%
21		-3.13%	-3.13%
22		5.45%	5.45%
23		0.93%	0.93%
24		0.56%	0.56%
25		-2.97%	-2.97%
26		-0.10%	-0.10%
27		-0.57%	-0.57%

Week No.	BUY	SELL	Buy & Hold
27		0.57%	0.57%
28		2.57%	2.57%
29		0.99%	0.99%
30		2.72%	2.72%
31		-2.50%	-2.50%
32		3.88%	3.88%
33	6.53%		6.53%
34	1.55%		1.55%
35		3.72%	3.72%
36		-0.38%	-0.38%
37		4.62%	4.62%
38		1.20%	1.20%
39		3.59%	3.59%
40		-0.99%	-0.99%
41		6.33%	6.33%
42		2.57%	2.57%
43		1.85%	1.85%
44		-13.58%	-13.58%
45		1.37%	1.37%
46		-5.60%	-5.60%
47		3.56%	3.56%
48		6.97%	6.97%
49		0.77%	0.77%
50		1.04%	1.04%
51		4.76%	4.76%
52	7.15%		7.15%
53	3.88%		3.88%
Averages	2.71%	-0.86%	-0.28%

Figures from: 12/31/2010 to: 12/28/2017

144

HISTORICAL YEARLY RETURNS

Year	Market Value		Annual Returns		Win
	Buy & Hold Strategy	Trading Strategy	Buy & Hold Strategy	Trading Strategy	
2010	$ 10,000	$ 10,000	0%	0%	Y
2011	$ 5,193	$ 8,832	-48%	-12%	Y
2012	$ 2,911	$ 14,776	-44%	67%	Y
2013	$ 145	$ 16,945	-95%	15%	Y
2014	$ 59	$ 20,334	-59%	20%	Y
2015	$ 13	$ 50,400	-78%	148%	Y
2016	$ 20	$ 66,677	57%	32%	N
2017	$ 21	$ 111,319	4%	67%	Y
Averages	-	-	-32.9%	42.2%	87.5%

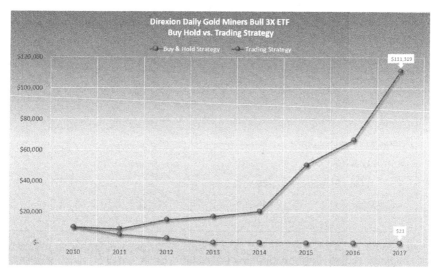

145

DIREXION DAILY GOLD MINERS BEAR 3X ETF (DUST)

SUMMARY

Ticker: DUST

Description: The investment seeks daily investment results, before fees and expenses, of 300% of the inverse (or opposite) of the performance of the NYSE Arca Gold Miners Index. The fund, under normal circumstances, creates short positions by investing at least 80% of its assets in: futures contracts; options on securities, indices and futures contracts; equity caps, floors and collars; swap agreements; forward contracts; short positions; reverse repurchase agreements; exchange-traded funds ("ETFs"); and other financial instruments that, in combination, provide inverse leveraged and unleveraged exposure to the NYSE Arca Gold Miners Index. The fund is non-diversified.

Data From: 1/3/2011 To: 12/28/2017		Total Return		
Winning Probability		• Buy & Hold:		-97.52%
• Monthly:	92.86%	• Trading Strategy:		-15.09%
• Annually:	100.00%	Trading Weeks:		
		BUY		SELL
Average Annual Returns		6		33
• Buy & Hold:	-7.14%			
• Trading Strategy:	39.11%	36		52
• Delta:	46.25%			

⚠ NOTE: It is not advisable to be in short ETF's positions for a long period of time. Timing on Shorts are key to making a profit in a short amount of time. Frequently adjust your stop losses to ensure you lock in profits.

146

MONTHLY ANALYSIS

Month	Average Return Buy & Hold Strategy	Average Return Trading Strategy	Standard Dev of Month Return (Volatility)	Percentage Wins
Jan	-8.70%	0.20%	30.43%	71.43%
Feb	-7.14%	-5.78%	34.05%	85.71%
Mar	8.30%	8.30%	26.64%	100.00%
Apr	-0.88%	-0.88%	35.45%	100.00%
May	5.39%	5.39%	13.64%	100.00%
Jun	3.09%	3.09%	41.53%	100.00%
Jul	-0.44%	-0.44%	35.83%	100.00%
Aug	-11.70%	-1.25%	36.69%	85.71%
Sep	13.36%	13.28%	33.99%	85.71%
Oct	1.26%	1.26%	33.75%	100.00%
Nov	12.14%	12.14%	26.52%	100.00%
Dec	1.37%	11.09%	21.95%	85.71%
Averages	1.34%	3.87%	30.50%	92.86%

Figures from: 12/31/2010 to: 12/28/2017

WEEKLY AVERAGE RETURNS

Week No.	BUY	SELL	Buy & Hold
1		0.96%	0.96%
2		4.43%	4.43%
3		1.86%	1.86%
4		3.15%	3.15%
5		8.14%	8.14%
6	4.85%		4.85%
7	3.48%		3.48%
8	2.77%		2.77%
9	2.65%		2.65%
10	2.08%		2.08%
11	1.86%		1.86%
12	4.53%		4.53%
13	5.43%		5.43%
14	0.93%		0.93%
15	4.89%		4.89%
16	3.83%		3.83%
17	3.95%		3.95%
18	5.02%		5.02%
19	2.49%		2.49%
20	2.07%		2.07%
21	2.25%		2.25%
22	5.64%		5.64%
23	1.32%		1.32%
24	0.50%		0.50%
25	4.28%		4.28%
26	2.07%		2.07%
27	0.04%		0.04%

Figures from: 12/31/2010 to: 12/28/2017

Week No.	BUY	SELL	Buy & Hold
27	0.04%		0.04%
28	-3.06%		-3.06%
29	-1.03%		-1.03%
30	-4.19%		-4.19%
31	3.19%		3.19%
32	-5.40%		-5.40%
33		-8.45%	-8.45%
34		-2.68%	-2.68%
35		2.75%	2.75%
36	-0.22%		-0.22%
37	5.52%		5.52%
38	-1.65%		-1.65%
39	2.24%		2.24%
40	0.56%		0.56%
41	5.55%		5.55%
42	-3.82%		-3.82%
43	-2.39%		-2.39%
44	16.04%		16.04%
45	0.84%		0.84%
46	6.31%		6.31%
47	2.04%		2.04%
48	5.78%		5.78%
49	-0.34%		-0.34%
50	-0.33%		-0.33%
51	4.10%		4.10%
52		-7.33%	-7.33%
53		-5.11%	-5.11%
Averages	0.35%	2.82%	-0.23%

HISTORICAL YEARLY RETURNS

Year	Market Value Buy & Hold Strategy	Market Value Trading Strategy	Annual Returns Buy & Hold Strategy	Annual Returns Trading Strategy	Win
2010	$ 10,000	$ 10,000	0%	0%	Y
2011	$ 11,139	$ 11,303	11%	13%	Y
2012	$ 8,239	$ 16,776	-26%	48%	Y
2013	$ 23,036	$ 56,548	180%	237%	Y
2014	$ 12,896	$ 48,286	-44%	-15%	Y
2015	$ 8,639	$ 101,754	-33%	111%	Y
2016	$ 506	$ 7,668	-94%	-92%	Y
2017	$ 248	$ 8,491	-51%	11%	Y
Averages	-	-	-7.1%	39.1%	100.0%

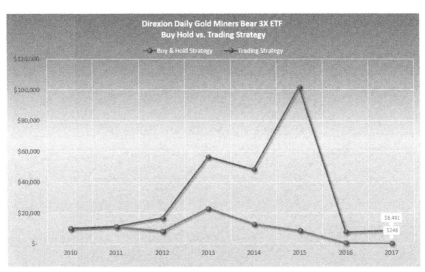

PROSHARES ULTRA CONSUMER SERVICES (UCC)

SUMMARY

Ticker: UCC

Description: The investment seeks daily investment results that correspond to two times (2x) the daily performance of the Dow Jones U.S. Consumer ServicesSM Index. The fund invests in securities and derivatives that ProShare Advisors believes, in combination, should have similar daily return characteristics as two times (2x) the daily return of the index. The index measures the performance of consumer spending in the services sector of the U.S. equity market. The fund is non-diversified.

Data From: 2/2/2007 To: 12/28/2017		Total Return		
Winning Probability		• Buy & Hold:		135.45%
• Monthly:	84.73%	• Trading Strategy:		1,518.27%
• Annually:	75.00%	Trading Weeks:		
			BUY	SELL
Average Annual Returns			6	1
• Buy & Hold:	16.09%		27	19
• Trading Strategy:	30.43%		43	39
• Delta:	14.34%			

MONTHLY ANALYSIS

Month	Average Return Buy & Hold Strategy	Average Return Trading Strategy	Standard Dev of Month Return (Volatility)	Percentage Wins
Jan	-8.44%	0.00%	16.28%	80.00%
Feb	2.81%	2.61%	9.55%	90.91%
Mar	5.90%	5.90%	8.80%	100.00%
Apr	3.99%	3.99%	7.67%	100.00%
May	-1.30%	0.20%	6.06%	54.55%
Jun	-3.70%	-0.53%	7.72%	63.64%
Jul	2.75%	2.75%	8.47%	100.00%
Aug	-1.61%	-1.61%	8.86%	100.00%
Sep	0.51%	4.13%	10.54%	81.82%
Oct	2.51%	1.96%	15.07%	45.45%
Nov	3.57%	3.57%	9.26%	100.00%
Dec	4.17%	4.17%	8.95%	100.00%
Averages	0.93%	2.26%	10.41%	84.73%

Figures from: 02/02/2007 to: 12/28/2017

WEEKLY AVERAGE RETURNS

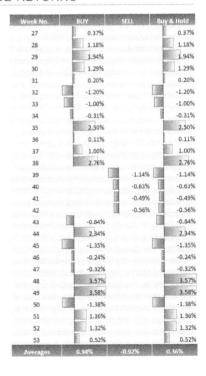

Week No.	BUY	SELL	Buy & Hold
1		-0.22%	-0.22%
2		5.94%	5.94%
3		0.93%	0.93%
4		0.85%	0.85%
5	0.00%	-0.11%	-0.10%
6	1.33%		1.33%
7	1.11%		1.11%
8	0.59%		0.59%
9	0.23%		0.23%
10	0.56%		0.56%
11	2.77%		2.77%
12	1.60%		1.60%
13	-0.41%		-0.41%
14	2.72%		2.72%
15	0.17%		0.17%
16	1.92%		1.92%
17	3.31%		3.31%
18	0.60%		0.60%
19		2.30%	2.30%
20		1.95%	1.95%
21		1.46%	1.46%
22		0.87%	0.87%
23		0.78%	0.78%
24		-0.13%	-0.13%
25		0.71%	0.71%
26		0.00%	0.00%
27	0.37%		0.37%

Figures from: 02/02/2007 to: 12/28/2017

Week No.	BUY	SELL	Buy & Hold
27	0.37%		0.37%
28	1.18%		1.18%
29	1.94%		1.94%
30	1.29%		1.29%
31	0.20%		0.20%
32	-1.20%		-1.20%
33	-1.00%		-1.00%
34	-0.31%		-0.31%
35	2.50%		2.50%
36	0.11%		0.11%
37	1.00%		1.00%
38	2.76%		2.76%
39		-1.14%	-1.14%
40		-0.63%	-0.63%
41		-0.49%	-0.49%
42		-0.56%	-0.56%
43	-0.84%		-0.84%
44	2.34%		2.34%
45	-1.35%		-1.35%
46	-0.24%		-0.24%
47	-0.32%		-0.32%
48	3.57%		3.57%
49	3.58%		3.58%
50	-1.38%		-1.38%
51	1.36%		1.36%
52	1.32%		1.32%
53	0.52%		0.52%
Averages	0.94%	-0.92%	0.36%

HISTORICAL YEARLY RETURNS

Year	Market Value Buy & Hold Strategy	Market Value Trading Strategy	Annual Returns Buy & Hold Strategy	Annual Returns Trading Strategy	Win
2006	$ 10,000	$ 10,000	0%	0%	Y
2007	$ 7,416	$ 7,491	-26%	-25%	Y
2008	$ 2,914	$ 7,072	-61%	-6%	Y
2009	$ 4,798	$ 13,446	65%	90%	Y
2010	$ 7,011	$ 23,723	46%	76%	Y
2011	$ 7,542	$ 27,422	8%	16%	Y
2012	$ 11,202	$ 36,321	49%	32%	N
2013	$ 22,143	$ 59,199	98%	63%	N
2014	$ 28,223	$ 90,776	27%	53%	Y
2015	$ 30,626	$ 98,942	9%	9%	Y
2016	$ 33,043	$ 122,032	8%	23%	Y
2017	$ 23,545	$ 161,827	-29%	33%	Y
Averages	-	-	16.1%	30.4%	75.0%

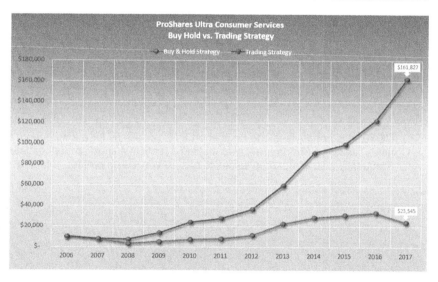

ProShares Ultra Consumer Services
Buy Hold vs. Trading Strategy

SUMMARY

Ticker: VIX

Description: CBOE Volatility Index, a popular measure of the implied volatility of S&P 500 index options; the VIX is calculated by the Chicago Board Options Exchange (CBOE). Often referred to as the fear index or the fear gauge, the VIX represents one measure of the market's expectation of stock market volatility over the next 30-day period.

Data From: 1/2/1990 To: 12/28/2017		Total Return	
Winning Probability		• Buy & Hold:	-40.95%
• Monthly:	66.37%	• Trading Strategy:	170,649.84%
• Annually:	86.21%	Trading Weeks:	
		BUY	SELL
Average Annual Returns		4	6
• Buy & Hold:	3.29%	18	21
• Trading Strategy:	38.88%		
• Delta:	35.59%	30	42

⚠ NOTE: It is not advisable to be in short ETF's positions for a long period of time. Timing on Shorts are key to making a profit in a short amount of time. Frequently adjust your stop losses to ensure you lock in profits.

MONTHLY ANALYSIS

Month	Average Return Buy & Hold Strategy	Average Return Trading Strategy	Standard Dev of Month Return (Volatility)	Percentage Wins
Jan	0.89%	5.26%	16.98%	67.86%
Feb	3.19%	-0.54%	18.90%	35.71%
Mar	-1.44%	0.00%	14.45%	64.29%
Apr	-3.21%	0.00%	14.47%	60.71%
May	1.76%	5.46%	17.50%	64.29%
Jun	-2.15%	0.00%	15.52%	64.29%
Jul	8.59%	9.96%	24.24%	64.29%
Aug	8.47%	8.47%	30.91%	100.00%
Sep	5.94%	5.94%	20.63%	100.00%
Oct	1.76%	2.59%	22.07%	50.00%
Nov	-4.27%	0.00%	15.40%	64.29%
Dec	-0.26%	0.00%	15.14%	60.71%
Averages	1.61%	3.09%	19.55%	66.37%

Figures from: 01/02/1990 to: 12/28/2017

WEEKLY AVERAGE RETURNS

Week No.	BUY	SELL	Buy & Hold
1		-1.68%	-1.68%
2		-1.17%	-1.17%
3		-3.71%	-3.71%
4	1.02%		1.02%
5	-2.19%		-2.19%
6		0.52%	0.52%
7		-5.09%	-5.09%
8		-1.53%	-1.53%
9		-0.93%	-0.93%
10		-2.74%	-2.74%
11		-1.17%	-1.17%
12		-3.41%	-3.41%
13		-0.21%	-0.21%
14		-1.12%	-1.12%
15		-3.41%	-3.41%
16		-1.99%	-1.99%
17		-3.80%	-3.80%
18		-2.71%	-2.71%
19	4.99%		4.99%
20	-0.19%		-0.19%
21		-2.65%	-2.65%
22		-4.70%	-4.70%
23		-1.93%	-1.93%
24		-1.43%	-1.43%
25		-2.10%	-2.10%
26		-0.60%	-0.60%
27		-3.94%	-3.94%

Week No.	BUY	SELL	Buy & Hold
27		-3.94%	-3.94%
28		-3.10%	-3.10%
29		-4.54%	-4.54%
30	0.21%		0.21%
31	2.66%		2.66%
32	2.53%		2.53%
33	-0.81%		-0.81%
34	2.19%		2.19%
35	-0.68%		-0.68%
36	-2.61%		-2.61%
37	-0.23%		-0.23%
38	-2.70%		-2.70%
39	1.64%		1.64%
40	-2.57%		-2.57%
41	1.12%		1.12%
42		-0.18%	-0.18%
43		-0.37%	-0.37%
44		-2.28%	-2.28%
45		-0.41%	-0.41%
46		-0.98%	-0.98%
47		-5.05%	-5.05%
48		0.41%	0.41%
49		-5.79%	-5.79%
50		4.54%	4.54%
51		-6.21%	-6.21%
52		-1.98%	-1.98%
53		4.85%	4.85%
Averages	0.13%	-1.98%	-1.34%

Figures from: 01/02/1990 to: 12/28/2017

153

HISTORICAL YEARLY RETURNS

Year	Market Value		Annual Returns		Win
	Buy & Hold Strategy	Trading Strategy	Buy & Hold Strategy	Trading Strategy	
1989	$ 10,000	$ 10,000	0%	0%	Y
1990	$ 15,302	$ 21,986	53%	120%	Y
1991	$ 11,201	$ 19,967	-27%	-9%	Y
1992	$ 7,291	$ 30,919	-35%	55%	Y
1993	$ 6,763	$ 42,244	-7%	37%	Y
1994	$ 7,657	$ 52,598	13%	25%	Y
1995	$ 7,262	$ 55,795	-5%	6%	Y
1996	$ 12,135	$ 45,978	67%	-18%	N
1997	$ 13,927	$ 52,471	15%	14%	N
1998	$ 14,165	$ 142,991	2%	173%	Y
1999	$ 14,292	$ 161,773	1%	13%	Y
2000	$ 15,574	$ 251,388	9%	55%	Y
2001	$ 13,805	$ 332,840	-11%	32%	Y
2002	$ 16,601	$ 255,944	20%	-23%	N
2003	$ 10,621	$ 267,302	-36%	4%	Y
2004	$ 7,709	$ 334,181	-27%	25%	Y
2005	$ 7,001	$ 535,918	-9%	60%	Y
2006	$ 6,705	$ 435,731	-4%	-19%	N
2007	$ 13,051	$ 436,625	95%	0%	N
2008	$ 23,202	$ 1,016,728	78%	133%	Y
2009	$ 12,575	$ 881,167	-46%	-13%	Y
2010	$ 10,296	$ 1,353,954	-18%	54%	Y
2011	$ 13,573	$ 3,764,783	32%	178%	Y
2012	$ 10,452	$ 4,576,717	-23%	22%	Y
2013	$ 7,958	$ 5,755,022	-24%	26%	Y
2014	$ 11,137	$ 14,453,789	40%	151%	Y
2015	$ 10,563	$ 20,157,327	-5%	39%	Y
2016	$ 8,144	$ 15,358,912	-23%	-24%	N
2017	$ 5,905	$ 17,074,984	-27%	11%	Y
Averages	-	-	3.3%	38.9%	86.2%

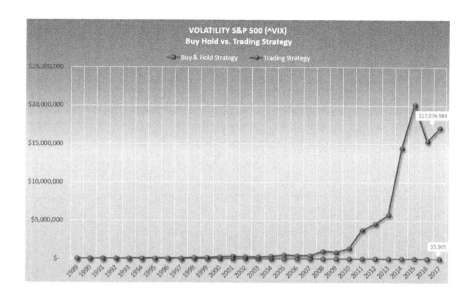

38327264R00089

Made in the USA
Middletown, DE
07 March 2019